Praise for
The Courage to Advance

"One cannot help but be inspired by the courage, humility, and tenacity of the special women profiled in these stories."

—**Christian Brickman, CEO of Sally Beauty Holdings**

"Women's empowerment is the single biggest opportunity of the 21st century. Read this book and be inspired by the courageous stories of those who are re-writing the rules of leadership."

—**Paul Polman, former CEO of Unilever PLC; cofounder & chair of IMAGINE**

"It's often through hearing the stories of others that we come to the best moments of clarity in our own. Women leaders are courageous, resilient, fully capable of making sense and success of the world around them. We adapt, and we also lead change. All, with grace, humility, and vulnerability. In this book are thirty-six stories of proof."

—**Coco Brown, founder & CEO of Athena Alliance, Inc.**

"*The Courage to Advance* will inspire you to never give up and to achieve more than you could have ever imagined!"

—**Dimitri Panayotopoulos, board director & former vice chairman of The Procter & Gamble Company**

"If you are ready for your head to be full of ideas, your heart running over, and your insides raring to go, *The Courage to Advance* is for you!"

—**Nanette Harrell, Independent Fractional Chief Information Officer & former Transportation Executive, Faneuil, Inc.**

"Remarkably elegant advice on how women have overcome societies innate obstacles to achieving their full potential in leadership without selling out on family and work-life balance. This book really helps our world on a path to gender neutral leadership. The stories told will give you courage, inspiration and the confidence to help you navigate the rocks, stones and jerks in the road."

—**Chris Perry, President, Broadridge Financial Solutions, Inc.**

"There is no single background, style, or path to become a successful leader. As seen in *The Courage to Advance*, one often has to overcome challenging systemic and interpersonal obstacles. Through hard work, clarity of purpose, and perseverance we see examples of women who are making significant, positive impacts on people and organizations. An inspiring read with useful words of wisdom for any leader.

—**Ken Pasternak, executive educator; keynote speaker; author**

"This book offers a compendium of advice from truly accomplished women leaders who shine a light on the executive path to success that often is hidden from sight. Part memoir, part guide to business, and part life advice, [*The Courage to Advance*] should stick to any serious reader who is looking for a path to succeed on their terms."

—**Dr. Anita Gupta, distinguished physician; author; FDA adviser**

"This book serves as a wonderful reminder that courage takes many forms. If ever there was an assembly of gutsy, talented leaders with inspiring stories, this is it!"

—**Jordan Rich, WBZ Radio Boston; podcast host; author**

"A great collection of strong, powerful, and easy-to-read stories from women leading business to the place it belongs. Value and beliefs are the main stimulants of quality leadership, and this book demonstrates in a humble way through real-life examples how these two factors can help to not only achieve business goals but also contribute to a better world."

—**Ali Ahmadian, CEO of Heliospectra**

"The courage demonstrated in the stories of these exceptional women serve as a reminder to us all to aim for the stars, even in the face of adversity."
—Dr. JJ Walcutt, scientist; author; CEO of Clay Strategic Designs; former Director of Innovation at the US Dept. of Defense; former US Democratic presidential candidate

"The wisdom from experiences that led these women to step fully into the light of their success is a gift to the reader and a road map for stepping into one's own power and potential."
—Rebekah E. Dopp, founder & chair of Exponent

"The book presents a moving account of the courage and resilience of these strong women leaders from all walks of life. These poignant portraits will stay with you long after you've finished reading."
—Charlotte Dennery, CEO of BNP Paribas Personal Finance

"Stories like these, brilliantly curated by Hagemann and Pent, will be pivotal in galvanizing the next generation of leaders. A must-read for every aspiring young woman."
—Carmen Ene, CEO of 3stepIT & BNP Paribas 3 Step IT

"This book will call you out, lift you up, and help you thrive in your purpose. A great how-to on leadership for those looking to take things to the next level."
—Sherrese Smith, partner at Paul Hastings; board member of Cable One, Norton LifeLock, America's Public Television Stations

"*Courage to Advance* brings the power of story front and center to educate and inspire the next generation of leaders"
—Shellye Archambeau, author of *Unapologetically Ambitious*; board member of Verizon, Nordstrom, and Roper Technologies

"Hagemann and Pent artfully weave together a narrative of empowerment and resilience in share-your-story format. In the spirit of being *'judged by the company you keep,'* those who read this work are keeping very good company."

—**Cathy Benko, Nike board member; former**
vice chairman of Deloitte LLP

"Some may pass over *Courage to Advance* simply because its title doesn't seem to resonate with them personally; they do so at their own peril! What's evident from the start is that these are REAL stories that have the power to immediately draw one in and then inspire and then teach! THAT is a combination to lean in to for growth!"

—**Julie Laulis, chair of the board & CEO of Cable ONE**

"This is a much-needed, inspirational, multicultural road map of how thirty-six extraordinary women leaders got to where they are. We need more examples to show to our young girls and emerging leaders of the grit, resilience, and pure creativity women needed when they came up against the expected norms set by their societies. Simply inspirational."

—**Muna AbuSulayman, Social Impact Investor; Philanthropist;**
Global Equity board member & adviser for Gucci

"These stories contain big lessons in bite-size pieces [and] show courage, resiliency, adaptability, sensemaking, and vulnerability at work. [*The Courage to Advance*] should be on the top of your desk, the lessons very much top of mind."

—**Andrew R. Hoehn, senior vice president**
of the RAND Corporation

"*The Courage to Advance* offers engaging leadership lessons, tips, and reminders—all through the power of storytelling!"

—**Aicha Evans, CEO at Zoox; board member**
for SAP & Joby Aviation

The Courage to Advance

Real life resilience from the world's most
successful women in business

BONNIE HAGEMANN, LISA PENT, AND THE MEMBERS OF WOMENEXECS ON BOARDS

NICHOLAS BREALEY
PUBLISHING

BOSTON · LONDON

First published in 2021 by Nicholas Brealey Publishing
An imprint of John Murray Press

A Hachette UK company

26   25   24   23   22   21   1   2   3   4   5   6   7   8   9   10

A CIP catalogue record for this title is available from the British Library

Library of Congress Control Number: 2021934774

ISBN 978-1-529-36899-4
US eBook ISBN 978-1-529-37607-4
UK eBook ISBN 978-1-529-36902-1

Printed and bound in the United States of America.

John Murray Press policy is to use papers that are natural, renewable, and
recyclable products and made from wood grown in sustainable forests.
The logging and manufacturing processes are expected to conform to
the environmental regulations of the country of origin.

John Murray Press Ltd   Nicholas Brealey Publishing
Carmelite House   Hachette Book Group
50 Victoria Embankment   53 State Street
London EC4Y 0DZ   Boston, MA 02109, USA
Tel: 020 3122 6000   Tel: (617) 263 1834

www.nbuspublishing.com

Every person who has ever done anything
meaningful has done it in the midst of
challenge, struggle, and pain.

If you're struggling,
you are not alone, and...
there is hope ahead.

CONTENTS

CHAPTER 3: ADAPTABILITY

CHAPTER 4: SENSEMAKING

CHAPTER 5: VULNERABILITY

ACKNOWLEDGMENTS

This book is brought to you not just by the authors and members of the WomenExecs on Boards network but by a dedicated team who worked many long, hard hours right in the middle of the 2020 pandemic and holiday season to offer you stories that are meant to bring you hope and inspiration when we all need a little more of each. Thank you to this amazing team of professionals:

Sara Bratcher, WomenExecs on Boards Network Administrator
Amy Sullivan, EDA, Inc. Chief of Staff
Gian Colombo, EDA, Inc. Creative Director
Corey Gilmore, Real Life, Real Leaders Podcast Producer
David Pinti, EDA, Inc. Media Production Intern
Riya Pujara, MA, EDA, Inc. Intern & Proofreader

Iain Campbell, Publishing Director at Hachette UK
Holly Bennion, Editorial Director, NB Publishing at Hachette UK
Michelle (Morgan) Surianello, Senior Production and Operations
    Manager at Hachette Book Group
Emily Frisella, Editorial Assistant, NB Publishing at Hachette UK

Melissa Carl, Sales Manager, Nicholas Brealey North America
Sarah Orthman, Marketing Executive, Nicholas Brealey North
    America
Lily Bowden, Marketing Executive, NB Publishing at Hachette UK
Helen Windrath, Contracts Manager at Hachette UK

Photo credits: photo of Ainslie Simmonds © Ainslie Simmons; photo of Annabelle Vultee © Annabelle Vultee; photo of Arti Singh © Arti Singh; photo of Bhavani Amirthalingam © Bhavani Amirthalingam; photo of Bonnie Hagemann © Brian Paulette; photo of Chris Cheeseman © Chris Cheeseman; photo of Christine Fellowes © Christine Fellowes; photo of Cinny Murray © Chicos; photo of Dorlisa Flur © Dorlisa Flur; photo of Elaine Dorward King © Elaine Dorward King; photo of Emmanuelle Mace Driskill © Emmanuelle Mace Driskill; photo of Gisella Benavente © Gisella Benavente; photo of Hana'a AlSyead © Hana'a AlSyead; photo of Heidi Zuckerman © Heidi Zuckerman; photo of Iram Shah © Iram Shah; photo of Jeanine Charlton © Jeanine Charlton; photo of Joanna Massey © 2018, Joanna Dodd Massey; Photo Credit: Stephanie Simpson, Simpson Portraits; photo of Jocelyn Martin Leano © Jocelyn Martin Leano; photo of Judy Lee © David Tan; photo of Laura Kiernan © Laura Kiernan; photo of Lisa Pent © Lisa Pent; photo of Lynda Bourque Moss © Lynda Bourque Moss; photo of Marcia Garcia Nielsen © Christian Nielsen; photo of Nicole Parent Haughey © Nicole Parent Haughey; photo of Patricia Christian © Patricia Christian; photo of Patricia Fortier © Patricia Fortier; photo of Patricia Hurter © Kelly Fitzsimmons Photography; photo of Riv Goldman © Riv Goldman; photo of Roberta Sydney © Roberta Sydney; photo of Rosie Bichard © Rosie Bichard; photo of Saniye Gulser Corat © Saniye Gulser Corat; photo of Shing Pan © Shing Pan; photo of Sonja Vodusek © Sonja Vodusek; photo of Suzanna de Baca © Suzanna de Baca; photo of Virginia Parker © Virginia Parker

We dedicate this book to the unnamed and unrecognized
women who have gone before us to make a way for
the women in this book to be leaders and influencers
all across the world.

FOREWORD

In our professional roles at Harvard Business School, we have the privilege of getting to know some of the world's brightest and most accomplished executives—in the classroom, at various events, and through our research. The authors of this book, who attended the "Women on Boards: Succeeding as a Corporate Director" executive education course at HBS, are glowing examples of the kind of remarkable leader with whom we get to build relationships, and by whom we continue to be inspired. Bonnie Hagemann, Lisa Pent, and their colleagues in the WomenExecs on Boards network came to Harvard Business School to get an education, and they left with a mission to change the world.

The issue of gender parity in leadership positions is a complex one that deserves rigorous and sustained attention. Both of us are passionate about bringing the insights of gender research to people who can use those lessons to create real change in their companies and in society. Together, we coauthored *Glass Half Broken: Shattering the Barriers That Still Hold Women Back at Work* (Harvard Business Review Press, 2021), with the goal of helping organizations dismantle the barriers that keep women from advancing. With colleagues at HBS, we helped to found the school's Gender Initiative in 2015, where Colleen serves as director and where Boris is a faculty affiliate. Boris also co-chairs the "Women on Boards" course and teaches an MBA course on gender at work. We've authored and coauthored numerous articles and case studies on the state of gender in the workplace and on the career paths of women leaders. The courage, resiliency, and perseverance of the leaders profiled in this volume demonstrate what we have known for years: companies and industries need more women at the top.

Our experience studying leadership and organizations, and working directly with executives to help them develop and foster talent in their companies, has made it clear to us that women who have ascended to senior ranks have a critical role to play in fostering gender equity. The female leaders in the following pages provide inspiration for other women, whether emerging or established in their careers, who too often see very few role models who share their gender. They also provide important insight to all readers, regardless of gender, about the obstacles that women navigate in pursuit of their aspirations. The proverbial ladder of corporate success remains more difficult for women to climb. In the following pages, women who are incredibly successful by any measure are courageous enough to tell the messier parts of their stories— the challenges, the frustrations, and the hurdles they had to overcome to attain the heights they've reached. Together, they offer an honest look at the complexities of life and work and what it takes to keep moving forward in the face of adversity. There are lessons to be learned from these career journeys, but perhaps more importantly there is solace to be taken in knowing that everyone struggles—even those who appear to have it all. This book is a call to other leaders to find their inner strength and persevere, and to appreciate that everyone around them has had to do the same.

"When you make it to the top, turn and reach down for the person behind you." This exhortation, often attributed to Abraham Lincoln, is carried out faithfully by the team behind this remarkable book. They have normalized struggle and setbacks for current and future leaders, and in so doing inspired compassion for ourselves and others. That compassion and encouragement is exactly what women deserve as they grow, rise, and reach for the top.

Colleen Ammerman and Boris Groysberg
Harvard Business School
Authors of *Glass Half Broken: Shattering the Barriers That Still Hold Women Back at Work*

PREFACE

Sometimes there are stories that impact us in a way that helps us reframe our situation or causes us to change or inspires us to do something we weren't sure we had the courage to do. The late Susan A. Brock, PhD, lived a life that was one of those stories, the kind of story that inspires others and impacts lives, many lives. She was a consulting psychologist and led a Minneapolis-based management consulting firm. She was also an expert in psychological preferences and eventually created FLEX Care®, a program based on an understanding of fundamental differences in individual personalities for healthcare professionals. She once told the story of why she created it, in a graduation speech given to a large group of graduating medical residents.

Following her introduction, Dr. Brock walked onto the stage, tailored and polished from head to toe. She stood tall and proud before the graduates and looked across the audience, catching their eyes as she waited for silence. Then, she began to read her résumé. She listed achievement after achievement and degree after degree, until she had read all of the most pinnacle points of her life; and then she looked up as if awaiting their reaction but knowing that they were wondering what this had to do with them and their graduation. After a pause, she set down the paper and said, "Pretty impressive, huh?"

Next, Dr. Brock reached under the podium and pulled out a bag. She reached inside to pull out some facial wipes and began to wipe off her makeup. Once finished, she stepped back from the podium and out of her expensive high-heeled pumps to put on hospital slippers. She reached into the bag once more to retrieve a medical gown, which she put on over her tailored suit, and finally, she reached up and removed the beautiful wig she wore, revealing her smooth, bald head.

Standing before the graduates, now looking like the patient that she was, she told of her terminal cancer and how doctor after doctor had treated her, how they often spoke to her as if she were an unintelligent youth. Desiring to give them something that would last, she encouraged the soon-to-be physicians to see beyond the patient before them, to see the professional, the mother, the father, the laborer, the neighbor, daughter, friend, and sibling, and ultimately to speak to them as intelligent participants in their healthcare.

This story, like the stories in the book you are about to read, shows a person with great achievements, who others may at first assume to be lucky or rich or gifted or in some way out of reach; but behind what can be seen on the outside—behind every leader—there is great struggle, pain, sickness, tremendous work, and sacrifice. Learning about the struggles and how these leaders came through them can help you get up and keep getting up when you feel defeated or lacking in resources, support, finances, time, or energy. Even if you only have time to read one story on a bad day, this book can give you the encouragement to not give up and potentially so much more as you think about your own life and leadership.

The Courage to Advance is an inspirational leadership book that includes a powerful collection of stories about a specific group of women leaders as well as our thoughts on the leadership lessons revealed in the stories. It is intended to help women *and men* for generations to come, particularly for those who live in the gladiator world of business.

The women in these stories are powerful and internationally diverse and have impressive leadership accomplishments. They were brought together through one unifying experience: They have all completed the same course at the Harvard Business School, a course that has turned into a movement. In 2016, Harvard Business School offered the first-ever Women on Boards: Succeeding as a Corporate Director program. Program co-chair, Professor Boris Groysberg, shared that Harvard approved getting the program in the syllabus, and in the first class of 2016 there were 64 women from 18 countries. The criteria for acceptance included the following:

1. The attendees had to be senior businesswomen who hold or have held positions in large, established companies ranging from division head to CEO or those in senior executive roles who currently sit on nonprofit or private boards and who wish to serve on public corporate boards.

2. Each woman also had to have a nominating letter from a sitting CEO or board member for admission.

How the Authors Came Together

Bonnie Hagemann, coauthor of *Leading with Vision* and CEO of EDA, Inc., a top-of-the-house human capital firm, took an evening to create a database of the women who went through the 2016 and 2017 programs. When the database was complete, she sat back, blown away by the powerful seats these women held across the globe, convinced that if they banded together, they could change the world concerning gender equality in corporate leadership and governance, and she went to Lisa Pent with an idea for a professional network that has become an exciting reality.

Before the formation of the network and after completing the inaugural course, Lisa Pent, Global Head of Strategic Product Growth at Thomson

Reuters at the time and current Client Partner of Professional Services at Cognizant, held the participants together through bimonthly conference calls for continuing education and support. By mid-2017, and with the next year's class joining, they realized that not enough of the women were getting on corporate boards, and the network needed to do more to change that.

Together, they founded a formal network to bind these leaders together, use their connections to help one another, and to advance the state of women on boards, first for the network members and then to leave the ladder down and help others coming up behind them. Today, the formal WomenExecs on Boards network has over 190 members, from 23 countries, who are deeply committed to one another's success and who are working together systematically to create positive and lasting change for corporate governance and ultimately for the workplace. These women are the overcomers who will share their greatest successes, their most difficult obstacles, and how they faced them down to live and fight another day.

Connect and Follow

For questions and interaction with the authors, please reach out via the website or directly.

- Bonnie Hagemann via LinkedIn: https://www.linkedin.com/in/bhagemann/
- Lisa Pent via LinkedIn: https://www.linkedin.com/in/lisapent/
- WomenExecs on Boards: https://www.linkedin.com/company/womenexecs-on-boards

BONUS FOR THE READER

There are additional stories, full interviews, and packaged podcasts available for those who purchase the book on the website. Here is your access code: **36storieswithpower**. Website: www.couragetoadvance.com.

And…we have a special bonus section called "The Things We Couldn't Say," a compilation of incidents that the members of the network—both those in the book and those who are not in the book—stated happened to them but for multiple reasons do not feel they can share while they are still in the game.

How the book is Arranged

In every story there are clear successes and deep, behind-the-scenes struggles. In most of the stories, there are valuable leadership lessons. Some of the lessons we will call out as themes and share a few coaching and mentoring thoughts. The leadership themes we will focus on are:

Courage
Resiliency
Adaptability
Sensemaking
Vulnerability

There are other important leadership themes and competencies that show up throughout the book. Some that you will see in every story are *passion* and *hard work* and *grit*. We do not know of any leaders who make it to high levels without these three. There may be some, but we've never met them.

There are also some themes you will read about that are especially helpful during times of difficulty and disruption. One of them is *Creating a Compelling Vision and Engaging Others Around It*. We are living through such a disruptive point in history that we need leaders who will dare to imagine a bright future for their companies and then inspire others to lean in, roll up their sleeves, and help figure out how to get there. This type of visionary leadership gives us hope and helps us get through the times when there is no clear direction. It also requires all of the five characteristics that we cover in our themes, which is why we call them out and provide a short overview that we hope will help you as a leader.

Finally, you will see in each story what each leader felt were their highest achievements, followed by Stumbling Blocks or Stepping Stones. This is where you will read the story of at least one of their greatest struggles. The heading is a part of a longer quote, from Friedrich Nietzsche: "There will always be rocks in the road ahead of us. They will be stumbling blocks or stepping-stones: it all depends on how you use them." The last section is each leader's advice in their own words directly to you, the reader.

As you read the following stories, we hope that you will not only be inspired by these leaders but that you will also think about your own leadership and that you will take time to stop and really think about what you are reading. You can just enjoy the stories, or you can make them come to life by extracting the lessons, talking about them with others and drawing out what they mean in general and what they mean to you personally. However you choose to read the book, we hope that the following stories will help make the difference for you between staying down and getting up, one more time.

Chapter 1

Courage

"The credit belongs to the man who is actually in the arena, [...]
who spends himself in a worthy cause; who at the best knows in
the end the triumph of high achievement, and who at the worst,
if he fails, at least fails while daring greatly, so that his place shall
never be with those cold and timid souls who neither know victory nor defeat."

—Theodore Roosevelt

THE FOLLOWING STORIES HAVE AN underlying theme of courage: the
mental or moral strength to venture, persevere, and withstand danger,
fear, or difficulty.[1] Former 3M CEO George Buckley once said:

> Leaders make unpleasant decisions. They often face unpalatable
> choices.... Norm Coleman, our local senator (R-Minn.), asked
> me if it was right to bail out the automotive companies. I said
> it's not about good choices and bad choices but making choices
> that are bad or worse. I wish we weren't rewarding people for
> what they have done. But leaders had to choose between the
> unpalatable and the unthinkable. The unpalatable is supporting
> the banks. The unthinkable is the collapse of the banking system.
> Leaders aren't given the choice between dandelions and roses.
> It might be dandelions and chickweed. They are forced to make

choices with too little time and too little information. It requires courage and a strong stomach. I might be forced to make a decision in five seconds, which will then be studied for months by a team of 40 lawyers. The job that leaders have is difficult, and there are increasingly few people capable of doing it.[2]

Leadership requires courage, and it is not for the weak or the thin-skinned. Those who make their way up the leadership pipeline often do so by stepping out and stepping up. They take risks; they fail; they get up; they fail; they get up, and then they succeed.

In the stories that follow, you will read about leaders who immigrated to the United States, who bet their business on a deal, who blew the whistle on corruption, and many more who stood strong in the face of great adversity.

---

1. Merriam-Webster. (n.d.). Courage. In *Merriam-Webster.com dictionary*. Retrieved January 5, 2021, from https://www.merriam-webster.com/dictionary/courage
2. Jones, B. (2009, May 17). 3M CEO George Buckley focuses on leadership training. *USA Today Money Advice*. other, USA Today. https://usatoday30.usatoday.com /money/companies/management/advice/2009-05-17-buckley-3m-leadership_N .htm.

Surviving and Leading Through Extreme Circumstances

SANIYE GÜLSER CORAT

Director at UNESCO
Location: Greater Paris, France

MY HIGHEST ACHIEVEMENTS

1. First woman to successfully lead an Asian Development Bank (ADB) project-preparatory mission to design a $50 million income-generation project for veterans, mine victims, and women in Cambodia during a period in Cambodia's history when Khmer Rouge was still active in the countryside (1996–97). This was the first ADB loan project for Cambodia of this magnitude and scope.

2. First woman and first social scientist selected as a member of an international panel of experts by the World Bank to oversee the four-year process of drafting the Bangladesh National Water Policy and Management Plan (1999–2003). This was the first water policy in the world to integrate gender equality considerations.

3. First director for gender equality at UNESCO to make gender equality one of two global priorities of the organization in 2007; achieved gender parity in decision making (starting from 9 percent in 2004); established several flagship programs in education, the sciences, and media. Most recently, published two reports on artificial intelligence and gender equality that sparked a global conversation on gender bias in frontier technologies.

STUMBLING BLOCKS OR STEPPING-STONES

Interviewed by over 600 media outlets after commissioning the latest research, *I'd Blush If I Could*,[1] and the winner of the 2020 Women in Tech Global Leadership award, Saniye Gülser Corat is touching the world for gender equality. She is the epitome of an independent French woman who is beautifully comfortable with both her femininity and her power; but she isn't actually French, although she speaks the language fluently, along with English and Turkish. She grew up in Istanbul, Turkey, where she stayed until she attained her undergraduate degree in business administration and political science from Boğaziçi University. After that, Gülser spent a year studying European affairs at the College of Europe in Bruges, Belgium, and then moved to Ottawa, Ontario, Canada, to complete both a master's degree and a doctorate in political science from Carleton University.

Gülser's doctoral thesis was on rural development, and her studies took her to the Ivory Coast and Cameroon, in West Africa, to do her field research. She was studying political economy and learning from various villages, where she gathered information about the different forms of organization for agricultural production. And this is where her life took on a deeper purpose. During the process, she noticed that as she conducted her research, she always ended up talking to men. Officially perplexed, she finally inquired where the women were in these villages. They said that the women were working in the field and the men were the ones with the time to meet with her. Surprised by the statement, Gülser started to look at how labor was divided between men and women.

After her university studies, Gülser started her own international development consulting company, ECI Consulting, Inc. Her efforts bore fruit as she built the company, established a broad funding base, managing investments of over $50 million, forming and leading teams of over 150 international staff. The work influenced strategic decisions in international development and funding and provided innovative solutions to development issues around the world. As she led her company, Gülser became culturally fluent, eventually living and working in over 30 countries and on all continents. After her initial awakening to gender inequality, she made sure that there was an analysis of the gender relations included in every project. The work was often difficult, and while many assignments were dangerous, the one in Cambodia took the most out of her as a person and as a leader.

In 1997, she was leading a project-preparatory mission for the Asian Development Bank in Cambodia. While no longer in power, the Marxist leader Pol Pot and his brutal Khmer Rouge regime were still around. The country was emerging from a horrific time under his leadership during which their history was destroyed, their educated class executed, and their citizens starved and overworked. The country was in ruins. The Asian Development Bank wanted to give a $50 million loan to Cambodia to use for employment for people who were veterans. As the team leader, Gülser's mandate was to create a project that provided employment opportunities for three groups of people: the military veterans, the people with disabilities, and the women.

She and her team were to set up shop in a well-protected area in the capital city of Phnom Penh. They also had their own private guards, because Pol Pot and Khmer Rouge were still active outside of the city. To add to the complications, the country had practically no infrastructure. She was supposed to set up an office with one Cambodian young man, who was acting as her interpreter, because she didn't speak Khmer, the language of the country. Everything had to be imported. They had to negotiate with businesses to get a generator so they could have electricity in the office for the computers for her team. The computers had to be approved by the government. She had to build everything from absolute scratch. And, to top it off, there was no trust in the country: under Khmer Rouge, the people had to give each other up to survive, and as a result no one trusted anyone. She would negotiate to buy a generator and then the next week spend hours convincing a business owner to sell her the same generator he had already agreed to sell her the week before.

Traveling with her team to different regions, Gülser was a prime target for Pol Pot, so they had to go in government vehicles with security, and she had to travel in disguise. Due to the intense circumstances, her team became more needy than others she had worked with, so she also had to find the extra strength to lead them. They had to live together as a team, and to stay safe they had to move living quarters several times during her eight months in the country. It was very exhausting, both emotionally and physically.

Fortunately, Gülser has a very supportive spouse and partner in Tom Corat, who was a rock and a comfort throughout. He didn't live there with her, but they had an arranged call every three days for 15 to 20 minutes, and it was during these calls that she could let her guard down, often venting and in tears. He would tell her that she could quit and come home. That was a comfort, and it would somehow give her the strength to keep going. She also found a friend and confidant in the young man who was her interpreter.

The work was very important, because this was the first time any development agency or multilateral bank was going to give a special loan to Cambodia. She was the representative of the bank, and they were providing incomes that many people needed and relied on. They were also reestablishing infrastructure by setting up business incubators and educating the citizens.

When she felt like giving up, she would hear the words of her father, who taught her to aspire to a higher purpose than herself. His words solidified when a very poor Cambodian woman walked up to her with her three stark-naked kids in tow and explained that she had walked for 800 miles because she was told that the ministry would help her if she could get there. As she stood before the woman, she realized that if she didn't do this, no one would, so she pressed on. In terms of risk and reward, Cambodia was at the top of Gülser's list for both. It was one of the most difficult and continuously dangerous situations of her career. It took everything she had for eight long months where the days were long, the nights were longer, and where she slept with one eye open.

While successful as a business venture, the work itself began to wear her down. She worked in the poorest countries with people who had absolutely nothing. She wanted to help, and although her work contributed to each country and constituency group, the impact seemed small. Unable to fix or compartmentalize the often horrific living conditions she saw, Gülser began to internalize her stress. She became sick when she returned home from her trips and later began to get sick while still on the trips, ultimately having to be carried off an airplane on a stretcher. It was too much. She needed to make an impact in a different way.

When a position opened for the director of gender equality at UNESCO, Gülser applied. This is a specialized agency within the United Nations system established in 1945, in Europe, after the Second World War, with the objective to make sure that there was never another. Among 2,000 candidates, she made the final cut and was offered the position. She closed her business and took an influential seat on a global platform.

UNESCO's charge is to educate and create cultural dialogue in hopes that it will assist in positive progress and communication, and avoid future wars. At this writing, it is supported by 193 member states (countries) and is based in Paris, France. During her time there, Gülser championed programs and initiatives that promote gender equality. For the next 16 years, she was very influential in making gender equality one of two global priorities for UNESCO, convincing all 195 of the member states involved at the time to vote in consensus on the issue. Today, Gülser is stepping into new opportunities, including serving on corporate boards, where she will continue what has turned into her life's mission to advance the state of gender equality throughout the world.

Words of Wisdom from Gülser to You

- Stay focused and true to your personal values and principles. Nothing is worth selling your soul for.
- We need women who get to the top to continue to advocate for gender equality, as we find that many who get to the top stop advocating for fear of losing their stature. We must remember that any woman who has made it to high levels has done so on the backs of the women who have gone before them. They made a path, and we must take the path and create an even broader and more accessible path behind us. When you get to the top, don't forget to leave the ladder down.

---

1. Mark West, Rebecca Kraut, and Han Ei Chew (2019). I'd blush if I could: closing gender divides in digital skills through education. *UNESCO for the EQUALS Skills Coalition*. Available from: unesdoc.unesco.org/ark:/48223/pf0000367416 .page=1

Virginia Parker, CFA

Founder and CEO, Parker Global
Strategies
Location: Stamford, Connecticut,
United States

My Highest Achievements

1. As a woman-owned, independent boutique firm, became a well-known alternative investment manager in Japan, launching the first public fund of hedge funds (1998), the first collateralized fund obligation structure for a multi-manager strategy (1990), and the first US energy infrastructure fund (2008)
2. From a startup, eventually raised $3 billion in assets under management, operating in 15 countries, with offices in six
3. Using cutting-edge technology along with complex risk reporting, won one of the largest Japanese mandates, in 2005, competing against 98 other firms

STUMBLING BLOCKS OR STEPPING-STONES

Virginia (Ginny) Parker has a reserved yet warm demeanor. In a room full of strong leaders, you might not notice Ginny, until she weighs in on a topic and then you notice...because when Ginny speaks, everyone listens.

She is helpful and thoughtful and creative. Ginny will be in a meeting, and she will listen, often waiting until several dissenting opinions are on the table; and if you've worked with her before, you know she is not passively hoping this will go away. Instead, she is problem-solving; and when she does finally weigh in, her solution is often the end of the discussion, because she will have taken all the competing needs into account and then resolved many of the issues with one swoop and manage to resolve contentious issues without contention. Ginny's skills at resolving issues may be partially due to her intelligence and temperament, but those skills have been honed in the fire, as she has built a successful firm that provides institutional clients with alternative investment strategies, specifically hedge funds and infrastructure.

While Ginny's success and financial prowess are impressive, it isn't something that she fell into. She started early with an interest in the stock market at only 5 years old. She studied the stock market all through her youth, but after pursuing a bachelor's in economics and political science from Duke University, she found herself in the insurance industry. Compared to the market, insurance felt like watching grass grow. She knew she needed to find her way to the work she loved.

She watched and waited, and eventually she zeroed in on a gap in the market. She stepped out and started an exciting journey that has taken her all over the world, working with some of the highest financial powers and dealing with corporate and government leaders and officials. It's been quite a ride, but it didn't start with a lot of flair. Ginny started her business in December of 1996, with a blank sheet of paper to write her business plan and began raising money. Surprisingly, when she started raising capital and explained the firm's unique opportunity, some top traditional money managers didn't understand what she saw and wouldn't invest.

Rejection often turns weaker hearts back to the norm, but Ginny's heart isn't weak. She began to reach out to her contacts to gain access to large banks who wanted to outsource a portion of their foreign exchange trading. This wasn't Ginny's big idea, but it would pay the bills and ultimately help fund what she really wanted to do. When the potential clients saw what she could offer, the mandates rolled in, and Ginny was able to land several of the largest Canadian banks as clients as well as a major Canadian pension plan, but she still wasn't satisfied.

What she really wanted was to provide institutions access to hedge funds and diversified strategies so her clients would have complete transparency with continual risk monitoring of their portfolios. Other hedge funds were very, very secretive, and few of them were willing to provide information. She believed that if hedge funds were going to be a real business, that transparency, independent risk oversight, and diversified and strategic manager selection were going to be the most important factors for success.

She set out to fill this market gap, and soon her firm had an opportunity to go to Japan and to speak to IBJ Securities, a subsidiary of one of Japan's largest banks. IBJ liked what they heard, and they invited her back two weeks later over the US Thanksgiving holiday. They wanted to do a tour to every major institutional investor and some of the large brokerage firms throughout Japan. After this road show, Ginny and her team received a call that they had an order for a $600 million fund. Finally playing the game she had always wanted to play, she was over-the-top excited, but there was a caveat: Ginny had to come up with a bank that would provide a return of principal guarantee.

By this time, the Christmas holidays were in full swing, and very few investment banks were willing to take something like this on. Ginny ran through her network, talking to over 20 banks and finally found one—just one—willing to take it on. They wrote the term sheet the week between Christmas and New Year's.

Guarantor established, Ginny called the Japanese bank and let them know, and another road show was set for the end of January. Once she arrived, she and her team traveled all over the country, selling what would be the first retail hedge fund of funds that was ever offered in Japan. It was a very exciting time, and it was about to get more exciting... but not in a good way.

On the Friday before the road show, she was on the phone with the team that put together the term sheet and their risk management department. There were a lot of lawyers involved. It was a big conference call, and Ginny heard their risk manager say something that didn't make her very comfortable. Something was wrong, but she still had to get on the plane Saturday and go to Japan. Tuesday morning, at 4:30 a.m. in Osaka, she received a fax with a revised term sheet from the bank guarantor that essentially killed the deal.

Ginny advised the team, but the road show went forward. Knowing they had no guarantor, the team flew around the country, telling their story and pretending that everything was fine, because that's what they had to do to stay alive long enough to figure this out. Fortunately, there was a French bank that was quite interested in the deal. A few days later, the team had their first meeting with this French bank at 1:00 a.m., Friday morning. They stayed up all night and by the time the offices in Japan were opening Friday morning they had a new term sheet.

Ginny spent the next month in Japan working around the clock on the documentation. Her company's attorneys flew in from Chicago and the bank's attorneys flew in from France. With legal expenses quickly mounting, it seemed every two or three days the French bank would throw Ginny an impossible curve ball. She would have to negotiate again and again, and all this while working 20-hour days in smoke-filled rooms. Each hour ticked away thousands of dollars in expenses. In fact, the bills were getting so high that if they didn't get the deal done, they were out of business. Ginny had calculated the risk and bet the company on getting this deal through.

One of the requests was for Ginny's firm to get an enormous amount of Errors and Omissions insurance, so much that an insurance broker advised that there was not that much insurance limit in the entire world and certainly not for her small, independent company investing in hedge funds. However, when it was all said and done, Ginny and her firm sealed the deal as long as Ginny was willing to stay for the duration of the deal. The French bank was placing their bets on her. They trusted her. Her team trusted her, and her new clients trusted her. Ginny kept showing up and demonstrating that they could count on her to deliver.

Today, Ginny has been to Japan over 80 times and established wonderful, lasting relationships. She is a well-known expert, but Ginny is also a mother and wife, and her sacrifices have often included family. Like most working parents, Ginny has had to miss many holidays events, but she always tried to make it for the important event, even flying home from Europe for one night and returning the next, just so she could take her young son to get his teeth pulled.

WORDS OF WISDOM FROM GINNY TO YOU

- Look past the present and think about where you really want to be, and then try to figure out a road to get there. Figure out how to soar.
- The journey can be long, so be sure that you're taking enough time for yourself along the way, like getting exercise, spending time with family, friends, nature, or whatever helps you feel good to get your head clear.

MARIA DEL CARMEN GARCIA NIELSEN

Board Member and former CEO of Office Depot for Portugal and Spain
Location: Madrid, Spain, and New York, New York

MY HIGHEST ACHIEVEMENTS

- Built and successfully sold online Spanish language bookstore to Amazon, becoming a millionaire at 35
- Achieved position of Fortune 200 International Region CEO
- Named corporate board director for three privately held manufacturing companies

STUMBLING BLOCKS OR STEPPING-STONES

Maria came to the United States as an illegal immigrant at age 11. She was the youngest of six children born to Maria Teresa and Rufino Garcia, who wanted to send their children to the US to fulfill the American dream. It was a big dream and it required them to sacrifice their own desires and comforts for a long time. In the end, their plan, which now also relied on Maria's oldest siblings, took ten years of struggling, saving, and working extremely hard to set aside enough money to enable all the children, one by one, to move to the US from Perú in Latin America.

Before they left, Maria Teresa and Rufino Garcia instilled in each child the need for hard work, resilience, excellence, and their great fortune at the opportunity to go to the US. The only catch was that there still wasn't enough money for the parents to go as well, so by the time it was Maria's turn to move to Queens, New York, in the 1970s, she was mentally prepared, but had to do it alone.

The first siblings to move did not know anyone and did not speak English. They had to secure an apartment, work, and begin to find their way. Still, they managed to survive and send money home. Since Rufino wanted them to focus on learning English and excelling in the United States, Maria's sisters had to work secretly with their mother to devise a plan that wouldn't alert their father. They said they were learning English, but instead these young, well-educated women who had college degrees from Perú worked long hours in New York City factories and sent money home until there was enough to get all the siblings and their parents to the United States.

Because Maria was only eleven, she would soon be sent to St. Bartholomew's Catholic school for seventh and eighth grade and later Dominican Academy on 68th Street, between Park and Madison, for high school; but they arrived in January, and she couldn't attend school until September. For nine months, she had no parents and no school, but she held in her heart the American dream that her parents had instilled. Even at 11, Maria was determined. She told herself that she would repay her parents by making good grades and by becoming successful. Knowing that their part in this plan had been extremely difficult and that her part was to get good grades, she felt fortunate that her role was not as difficult as that of her parents and older siblings.

To help her learn English, Maria's brother enrolled her in karate, where her determination began to shine, as she not only began to speak a new language, but she also became a black belt. It was seven more years before she was finally able to become a US citizen at the age of 18, and by then she was well on her path to success. She did get good grades in school, just as she had promised herself, and she eventually received full scholarships to Cornell University and Wharton School of Business, where she received a bachelor of science (BS) degree in mechanical engineering and a master's in business administration (MBA).

Still, there has been an underlying internal struggle. Despite her youthful success and determination, Maria struggled with the counterposed desire to be authentic about her humble upbringing and the feeling of belonging amid polished second- or third-generation corporate leaders. At school, and early in her career, at her core Maria knew that her English wasn't perfect and that her family did not come from a legacy of wealth. However, her ability to outwork her peers, and the idea that she had been granted a lucky break by moving to the US, energized her to confront any challenge. As she has moved to senior leadership roles, and especially through her mentoring of younger, diverse talent, Maria better understood that nuances mattered and that, while trivial to some, those are all the signals that we send to others.

Reflecting back, she is glad that she was not always aware of her limitations. One example is her tenure as a strategy consultant for McKinsey & Company, a top global management consulting firm. McKinsey hires a specific type of person, which includes excellent academics, professional polish, and a strong network. Maria had the academics, but other than that, all she had to go on was how hard she worked and how motivated she was to continue learning. She pushed herself hard. If everyone else was doing X, then she would do X multiplied by 10.

Maria's hard work and determination paid off, as her career after McKinsey included an early dot-com-era internet startup called Libroweb, an online bookstore that anchored the Spanish book market for a European group of online stores. Libroweb was eventually acquired by Amazon, making Maria a millionaire in her mid-thirties. After that, her career continued to thrive, and she went on to become the CEO for Office Depot in Portugal and Spain, where she stayed until she left management to pursue corporate governance. She now spends her time working on corporate boards, including Lontana Group, FEGEMU a Portwest Company, and Grupo SANZ, all privately held industrial companies.

While wildly successful to most, Maria has never quite been able to shake the question of whether her first-generation college and immigrant self belongs, but she does not let that stop her from pursuing her dreams. She uses it to fuel her work ethic and her passion. She often shares with others how fortunate and grateful she is to have parents who were courageous enough to send her and her siblings to the United States. She continues, even to this day, to remember that she has been granted all these opportunities, and whenever she is given the chance, she works hard to excel.

WORDS OF WISDOM FROM MARIA TO YOU

- What I hope for you is that you will remember to recognize the support that you have and that you surround yourself with others who allow you to have success. When I look back at my own story—if I look back at that girl—I believe she should have been more generous with recognition. I didn't give enough recognition to those who helped me. Remembering it now, I'm so surprised and humbled that my family was still supportive of my career and celebrated my successes without asking for any recognition of the sacrifices that they had made. They were just there, cheering me on.
- I hope that as you read my story you will think about your own story and the others, because there are always others, who have helped you get to where you are. I also hope that you will remember your values, think about your place in this world, and decide what your legacy will be, because once you figure this out, you can let your values and purpose become your compass.

Heidi Zuckerman

Board Director, Podcast Host and former CEO
and Director of the Aspen Art Museum
Location: Aspen, Colorado, United States

My Highest Achievements

1. Successfully raising two amazing kids as a single mom while working full-time
2. Being one of four women in the United States to have raised over $100 million for a museum and one of three to have built a museum from the ground up (as of 2019)
3. Spending a career advocating for art and artists and creating channels such as a podcast and books and using social media to broadcast globally

Stumbling Blocks or Stepping-Stones

Heidi Zuckerman has a personal mission to connect as many people to art as possible and to share why art matters in daily life. She is clear and confident and extremely knowledgeable. She also seems to have an intuitive sense of what is needed both in the people she leads and in the art she shares. It's a knowing combined with a keen logic that she originally intended to use as an attorney and eventually a judge.

Heidi was born in New York, grew up in California, and went to Philadelphia for her undergraduate studies. She had known since she was young that she would eventually become a judge, so her career path was straightforward until the summer of her freshman year in college. She wanted a summer job, so she picked up a phone book and started going through the businesses that started with "A." An unusual way to change a career path, but that's exactly what happened. As she went through the A's, she soon landed on "art galleries," decided that sounded interesting, and called one art gallery after another from the top of the list until she landed a job in a gallery. Heidi had a combination of skills that proved helpful, and by the end of the summer she was basically running the gallery.

She was also introduced to art in a way that she hadn't been before. Even though her grandmother was an art collector, Heidi never thought about the art world as a career, but this experience changed her trajectory. She shared her new passion and plan for a career in the art world with her parents, who thought she wasn't thinking clearly. They encouraged her to take a summer, go to Europe, and get her head screwed back on straight and then come back and apply to law school. Heidi did go to Europe, where she spent the entire summer going to museums all around Europe and came back even more clear on what she wanted to do.

So, the shift was made. She continued her education at the University of Pennsylvania and added a work study at the Institute of Contemporary Art in Philadelphia. She was only sure about two things, she didn't want to teach art history or work in a museum, but once again she had an awakening and eventually did both. Today her life's work is educating others about art and its meaning, not just traditional art but the arts in a broader sense, which can include almost anything artistic, and of self-expression, including winemaking, graffiti, culinary arts, etc.

Along her career path Heidi learned both the for-profit and the not-for-profit side of the art world. She also learned that she had a knack for curating and leadership, and the two coalesced when she eventually took the CEO and director position at the Aspen Art Museum. There, her leadership skills were honed, and she also learned one of her hardest lessons of her career to date: things are not always as they seem.

One of the most exciting initiatives Heidi had was to build a new museum from the ground up. She jumped into the project, working closely with her board chair and the city. They found a property that belonged to the city that they initially offered for the construction of the new facility, but then the city changed the deal and said that in order to have the land, they would need to win a public vote. Completely surprised, Heidi and her team took a deep breath and began to prepare the strategy for a public campaign.

Eventually, they were able to secure a spot on the ballot, but they were art museum people, not politicians, and it turns out they were unaware of the some of the nuances of the community and its methods. Before the vote, Heidi and her team did everything they were supposed to do. They put out yard signs, registered voters, and got people to sign petitions and write letters. They also conducted polling, and according to the polls they had the vote by about 65 percent to 35 percent. So when election day finally came, they were ready to have an election victory party. Anxiously watching, they wrote the totals for each ballot initiative on a chalkboard. When the votes were tallied, Heidi saw the numbers on the board, and it was exactly opposite of her expectations. The vote was 67 percent no and 33 percent yes. Convinced that this must be an error and that they had mixed up the numbers, Heidi asked if they were inverted. They were not. The vote failed, and Heidi, her board chair, and her team were all blindsided and devasted.

Heidi spent the evening in tears of disappointment and frustration. How could they have been so wrong with the polling results? What had they missed? When she awoke the next day, all she really wanted to do was sell her house and leave Aspen, but she didn't. Once the shock wore off, she did a postmortem to figure out what happened. It turned out that the people in the community felt that public land should remain public land. The only problem was that the voters also didn't want to come out publicly and say that they were against the arts, so publicly they said they were for it, but when they cast their ballots, they were against it.

Heidi knew that she could leave the museum if she wanted to, and that was probably what helped her decide to stay. She still wanted to build the new museum. It wasn't an obligation. It was a desire. So, she pulled herself together and went back to the drawing board to create a new strategy. This time, she carefully sought out privately owned property in downtown Aspen. She approached the person who owned the property, which made the most sense, and they made a deal. Then Heidi went to the city and made a new deal with them. Three major steps down, she had already secured Pritzker Prize–winning architect Shigeru Ban Architects but still had to raise a lot of money. She did. After the new museum was built, annual attendance increased by 110 percent, staff tripled, and the number of students served by the museum's educational programming increased by a 1,140 percent. Heidi raised over $130 million during her tenure at the museum. Her most difficult career setback turned into her proudest professional accomplishment.

After the museum's future was secured, Heidi was ready to move on and today works to find ways to reach an even broader audience in her desire to connect people to art and its importance in daily life. She's proud of the work that was done and of her decision to stay and see it through despite such a devastating setback, and she's thankful that she learned so much in the process.

WORDS OF WISDOM FROM HEIDI TO YOU

- My shared experience is that you really need to trust the people that you work with, and you must be able to trust people through and through.
- Don't be afraid to end a relationship if you are not on the same page and you are unable to reconcile the misalignment.
- It's just really, really important to have the right people in the right roles.
- Don't let a false sense of pressure force you to decide too soon. Stop and pause: Take a breath, meditate, go for a walk, and get clear in your thinking. Then it's about responding to situations rather than reacting.

CHRIS H. CHEESMAN

Independent Board Director,
American Century Investments Equity
Mutual Funds and former Senior Vice
President and Chief Audit Officer at
AllianceBernstein
Location: Teaneck, New Jersey,
United States

MY HIGHEST ACHIEVEMENTS

1. At a young age, had significant global responsibility to assess enterprise-wide risks and controls and speak truth to power
2. Thrived at one company for 32 years, working for five different CEOs; during that span, successfully navigated the different cultures and strategic imperatives each new CEO brought to the firm; maintained impact and relevance. Led a global team through many periods of dramatic change and transition.
3. Most proud of being a diversity and inclusion champion well before it became in vogue. Excluding non-US team, built and developed the most diverse team in the entire company of over 3,000 people—diverse in every dimension, including age, race, ethnicity, religion, sexual orientation, and variably challenged and abled—a potent team.

4. Secured first board role three months prior to retiring. At the age of 45, decided to retire early (before age 60) while still relatively young and healthy and to bring her three decades of experience to use in the board room.

Stumbling Blocks or Stepping-Stones

Chris Cheesman is uncompromisingly professional. Excellence rings through every part of her work and persona. She is sharp, knowledgeable, articulate, and always prepared. She has a natural executive presence, but it is her performance that sets her apart and helped her reach the C-suite at a fairly young age. She has proven herself over and over throughout her career by consistently outperforming and exceeding expectations. Despite her role being one of critique, she became a trusted adviser, confidant, and thought partner on some of her firm's most complex problems.

Chris lives in New Jersey, but was born and raised in Staten Island, New York, and she considers herself a New Yorker at heart. She always wanted to be a teacher, but after getting a taste of corporate America from an internship at a wealthy insurance company during high school, she decided early on that she was going to pursue a successful corporate career. She obtained her bachelor's degree in accounting from Hofstra University in Long Island. She did well in school and as a result landed her first job out of the university at a top accounting firm, Pricewaterhouse.

While working, she secured her Certified Public Accounting (CPA) license. Chris didn't love this work and decided that she didn't want to stay in accounting and audit, but fate intervened. She had an opportunity to meet with several executives at what was then known as Alliance Capital Management (Alliance). At the time, the company had approximately $36 billion in assets under management (AUM) with 300 employees worldwide. Chris saw this as an opportunity to enter the global finance space, but she had no idea just how much of an opportunity it would turn out to be. Soon she had significant global responsibility reporting into the C-suite, building an international team and gaining influence in the company now known as AllianceBernstein, which today has approximately 3,900 employees with over $600 billion in AUM. She ended up staying for over 32 years.

While Chris was technically with one company for a long time, it really felt more like five different companies as it morphed with each new CEO. They each brought their own strategic imperatives and shaped the culture in new ways. With every shift in the landscape, Chris would pivot and find new ways to navigate both the organizational and market changes. She learned and grew continuously. As the chief audit executive her voice was heard and respected, and she built one of the most potent and diverse teams in the company. Very early on, she was at the table when Alliance went public and subsequently with each acquisition and growth initiative. She also demonstrated her willingness to go into uncharted territory. When offices around the world opened and/or expanded in Asia and Europe and/or the firm launched new products, Chris got involved.

One reason Chris is so respected is that she was not your normal check-the-box, compliance-type chief auditor. She understood the business and kept the business needs front and center. She was willing to speak truth to power and point out the problems when no one else would, which continuously increased her ability to influence across the organization. She didn't always want to be the lone voice pointing out issues, but she knew someone needed to; so even when she had some fear and trepidation, she kicked herself under the table and did it anyway. That was her job, and she had to do it well. She had a lot of responsibility.

The opportunities were incredible, but so were the challenges. As a young black woman learning to lead in a primarily white male corporate arena, she had more than her fair share of obstacles to overcome. It wasn't easy, and she also put a lot of pressure on herself. In fact, that was one of the more difficult parts of her career. She felt that failure was not an option. She wasn't just representing herself as a leader. She was representing women of color everywhere. There were perceptions that needed to be changed and differences that needed to be understood. She knew someone always must go first, and in her company, it was Chris. She felt she had to outperform, exceed expectations, and bring her A-game every single day. This underlying sense of responsibility resulted in a continuous, low-level anxiety that certainly went higher at times but never went away.

It was also lonely at times. There wasn't anyone around who looked like Chris who had her level of responsibilities and reporting lines. All the other executives, male and female, were white, and while cordially professional and collaborative, with the exception of a few, she always felt they didn't necessarily support her in the ways she observed them doing for others. She had a great rapport with most everyone, so she never sensed outright discrimination. It was more along the lines of implicit biases that we all have. However, there was one very senior leader who caused Chris a lot of grief. He constantly critiqued her work, her thoughts, and her opinions. It wasn't that she wasn't used to being critiqued or challenged, but this was like a tsunami, and for a period of time she began to doubt herself. She suffered from imposter syndrome. Despite all her success and every indication to the contrary, she doubted herself. For a moment she let it take her joy and her power, but it did not last. Eventually this individual left the organization, and Chris was still standing. She quickly recovered her confidence and continued her leadership journey.

A woman of faith, Chris made it through by trusting God through every step of her journey. She felt that beyond her day-to-day responsibilities, she had a higher purpose, and she often mentally recited her favorite scripture, "I can do all things through Christ Jesus who strengthens me."[1] But there was also another scripture that kept her going and still does to this day: "from everyone who has been given much, much will be demanded."[2] She feels very blessed in her life and therefore compelled to help others, particularly those who are marginalized, oppressed, or just in need. This calling served her well at Alliance, as time and again, just when she was at her wits end, someone would knock on her office door in need of help.

She was a mentor, a coach, a resource, and an encourager. This was

Chris's favorite part of the job, and it drew employees not only from her own team but also from different divisions and at different levels in the organization. She was also able to form lasting friendships during her tenure, and a network of support that is still in place even though she has moved into her well-planned early retirement to start the next phase of her professional career serving on corporate boards. Now she has a new calling, and the doors started opening even before she left, leading her to secure her first board seat a few months before her last day on the job. With her many years of experience and seasoned leadership, Chris doesn't feel the anxiety the same way she used to. She still has a lot to give, and she still brings her A-game, every day.

Words of Wisdom from Chris to You

- While mentorship and sponsorship are desirable, own your career journey.
- Unlike men, women sometimes find it hard to self-advocate, so I advise women to share, vocally and in writing, your accomplishments throughout the year. Everyone has bouts of self-doubt, but do not give those insecurities any power. Feel the fear and do it anyway!
- Never let anyone steal your joy or steal your power.
- Be the kind of leader that you've admired and that you would want to work for.
- Success is not a destination. It is a journey, so own your journey. Do not rely on someone else's help to make it happen for you.

---

1. Philippians 4:12–14 21st Century King James Version
2. Luke 12:48 New International Version

Suzanna de Baca

President and Group Publisher at
Business Publications Corporation,
Inc.
Location: Des Moines, Iowa,
United States

My Highest Achievements

1. As CEO, led a turnaround and subsequent merger of a multi-state Planned Parenthood affiliate to ensure continuity of services in a changing healthcare and regulatory landscape
2. Became president and part owner of a publishing company
3. Became a managing director at a Wall Street investment firm at the age of 34

Stumbling Blocks or Stepping-Stones

Suzanna de Baca's life has come full circle as the president of Business Publications Corporation, Inc., a media and communications company back in her home state of Iowa. She grew up in Iowa, and as a farm girl she was taught hard work, how to handle finances, the value of integrity, and a whole lot of common sense. She received her bachelor's degree in art and design from Iowa State University, pursuing a liberal arts path studying art history, religion, and anthropology. She was just really curious about how the world works and how everything fits together. She knew that she would pursue a graduate degree, but she had to work through college to pay for her education, so that would likely be down the road. Suzanna learned during her college jobs that the skills she gained on the farm were also called management skills. To her surprise, what she thought were common sense actions and decisions turned out to be skills in demand.

Once she graduated, Suzanna secured a position to run a nonprofit organization in Dallas, Texas. While she was running the nonprofit, she started to look at advanced-degree programs that would prepare her for more. She was considering arts administration, thinking she might want to run a museum someday, but there were three men on her board who had serious business backgrounds. One was a venture capitalist, one was a real estate investor, and the other a turnaround expert. They had noticed her management skills and told her that they thought she should get an MBA. Two of them had been to Harvard Business School, so they recommended that she apply.

Suzanna was surprised, as it seemed like a far stretch, but since she had done well in school and made excellent grades, worked, and had been a leader at her university—and her résumé was better than she realized—she decided to try it. To her surprise, she was accepted into Harvard Business School and her life leading and managing in business began. She never would have thought of herself as a corporate business leader if the men on her board had not opened her eyes to the possibility. She feels lucky and thankful that they did.

After she received her MBA, she took a position at an investment consulting firm that served institutional clients. She worked with endowments and foundations' portfolios. It was aligned with the work she loved both from a business and an art perspective, and she was very good at doing the job, which caught the attention of others. Soon she was recruited to do asset and investment management at a large Wall Street firm. She accepted and spent the next 20 years working primarily for investment firms leading teams and providing sophisticated wealth management strategies to various types of clients.

In one of the organizations, Suzanna started hearing colleagues in the hallway talking about engaging in illegal practices. She began to pay attention and listen closely, and soon it was clear: that was exactly what was happening. She went to leadership and shared what she had learned. Soon after, Suzanna started receiving threats, which she found out later was also happening to another woman in the firm, with the intent of pressuring them both out of the company. She recognized this as retaliation. She met with an attorney who said she had the right to take legal action, but she needed to think about whether she wanted to continue working for a place that tolerated compliance violations. She understood that if she fought, she would be taking on an organization with deep pockets, and if she stayed, she would be at a place that did not operate with integrity. Still, it was not an easy decision. It was a prestigious, high-level, and high-paying job. In the end she decided that she could not win one way or the other, so she resigned her position and left the company without a job and without a plan. She just knew she had to get out. Soon thereafter, the scandal broke, and her former company ended up in the news. Many were fired and the company paid steep fines. She was vindicated, but she still did not have a job or a plan.

It was a dark season in her life. She wondered if she had ruined her entire career. Even though she stood up for what was right, there was a stigma to being a whistleblower. She did not want to share too much with friends, because she was being threatened by this company. So she turned to books and meditation. She kept meditating on the situation and asking, "Why is this happening? What am I supposed to be learning?" Suzanna struggled for a while, but she has a depth, strength, and a determined spirit. She got back up and redesigned her entire life.

Having spent a lot of time thinking about what she wanted to do going forward, she knew one thing she wanted was more flexibility, so she decided to start her own business. During this time she also ended up reconnecting with someone she grew up with; they fell in love and eventually married. His love and support helped her continue to work through this transition. Life was looking up.

Before long, Suzanna's business skills drew attention again, and she was recruited to another large financial management business. She did her due diligence, successfully sold the company she had started, and took on this new challenge. After six years at that firm, she was ready for a change and was offered a position leading a region for Planned Parenthood in her home state, something completely different but exciting because it aligned with her values. She accepted the position and led the organization through a lot of political upheaval, defunding by the government, and business disruptions. She decided to merge the company with another and create a better solution for the long term, even though she knew she was working herself out of a job; but this time was different. She was making the decisions that were right for the organization, and the organization appreciated it. She also knew that she would be okay and that she would soon be running something else. And once she left, it was not long before she was the president at Business Publications Corporations.

In hindsight, the worst season of her life has led to the best season of her life so far. If it were not for the decision she made to follow her values, she never would have ended up in a long-distance relationship that turned into a new love and a new marriage. She never would have built a business for herself that she successfully sold, and she never would have ended up back in her home state leading businesses and serving communities through her work. And she did learn new things: She learned to dig deep into legal and ethical practices and history before joining a company or its board of directors; and she learned to ask questions about how a company would deal with questionable situations. So she did get answers to her meditations after all. The experience turned into an asset, and Suzanna now knows that she will stand up for her values in the face of great pressure and that she will get back up no matter how hard a punch life throws her.

WORDS OF WISDOM FROM SUZANNA TO YOU

- Take great care of yourself physically, spiritually, and mentally. Give yourself space and time to figure things out.
- Know yourself, trust yourself, and always be true to your values. It will all work out!
- No amount of money is worth it to feel like you are condoning something illegal or unethical.
- Get comfortable feeling a little uncomfortable and taking some risks.
- It is okay to fail. Everyone fails from time to time. Give yourself some grace. You do not have to be the best at everything. Resilience is a muscle, and failing, learning, and getting back up build the muscle.

Judy Lee

Cofounder and Managing Director, Dragonfly
CEO, Dragonfly Capital
Location: New York, United States; Asia

My Highest Achievements

1. Founded and built Dragonfly, a leading international risk management advisory firm over the last 20 years.
2. Pioneered quantitative risk management methodologies for banking. Built and implemented the first bank-wide risk capital system 30 years ago. Adopted by Basel in global bank capital regulations.
3. Grew a $1 billion renewable energy company within a traditional oil major, then founded a company to develop renewable energy power plants in Southeast Asia.

Stumbling Blocks or Stepping-Stones

Judy Lee is a first-generation United States citizen by birth, but her family has a longer history in the United States than others, extending back five generations. In 1867, her great-great-grandfather journeyed to the US from China and was among the early workers to build the Pacific–transcontinental railroad connecting America's east and west. It was the foresight and risk taking of Judy's great-great-great-grandmother who, forced by circumstances of being recently widowed, sold the family land for passage to send her son to America to rebuild the family fortunes. But at that time Chinese were not permitted to become citizens, so he would work hard for many years and then return to China. That was the pattern for multi-generations until Judy's father went to America and settled down. Judy was then born in Brooklyn, New York, the second of five children.

Her family came to the US with a dream, and in many ways, Judy's success is the fulfillment of that legacy. It doesn't take long watching Judy to know that the decades of their journeys back and forth and the long hours of hard labor have been worth it. She is a passionate New Yorker and a standout global citizen with homes in Asia and New York, serving on corporate and university boards, and advising CEOs on strategy and risk management of financial institutions and large corporates across industries. She is a published author and a dynamic and inspiring leader in our global network of some of the world's most influential women.

Judy is at once traditional and contemporary. While she is happiest when she is taking on new challenges and opening new avenues for growth, she closely identifies with her family, rooted in Confucian values of respect and community, never forgetting those who have come before her. This combination is one of her greatest strengths and one of her greatest struggles. She comes from a very traditional Chinese home where it is respectable to get a university degree, but there is not as much emphasis on careers for women as there is for men. Traditional expectations are for women to marry and have children, but that is where Judy's heart turned toward a different path.

Driven to achieve, Judy started working when she was 14 years old at Dynatron, a data-driven computerized marketing company. She majored in finance and international business at New York University Stern School of Business, graduating at 20 years old, and then went into the world of investment banking, working for Bankers Trust Company (later acquired by Deutsche Bank). This is where she faced another stereotype—she was young, female, and Asian. She had to find a way to have a voice and demonstrate that what she brought to the table was valuable. She began to break through early, working as a key member of the pioneering team that developed RAROC (Risk Adjusted Return on Capital), the risk quantification methodology that was later adopted by the Basel Accord global bank capital regulations.

She loved the challenge of business, the fast pace and the ability to help solve high-impact problems. At the same time, her family tradition implied an expectation to settle down. No one was saying it, but Judy felt it deep in her Confucian and Asian family roots. Nevertheless, Judy broke through the ingrained expectations of generations to sort out her direction and purpose.

While at Bankers Trust, Judy obtained her MBA from the Wharton School of Business, University of Pennsylvania. Later, she became a partner at two consulting firms focusing on strategy and risk management. She has a deep understanding of the way companies drive and sustain return on capital, and how important it is to analyze opportunities and risks over time instead of just focusing on the short term. Even after years of developing risk management frameworks, Fortune 500 companies were still making mistakes and suffering through spectacular failures that she knew could be mitigated with appropriate risk leadership and risk methodologies.

As she was analyzing companies and advising CEOs on risk management, she was simultaneously sorting out her own personal vision, strategy, and risks. Judy believes that we are here for a purpose, and she was determined to figure hers out. She spent time contemplating, meditating, and visioning. It seemed like a fork in the road, but she didn't accept the need to choose between her traditional family values and the drive inside of her to take the path less traveled.

Her personal purpose and family tradition came together when Judy remembered her grandmother's path. She was very close to her grandmother, who lived to be 105. When Judy's great-grandfather went to

America, he sent money back to his wife in China so that his daughter could get formal education. He was a man far ahead of his time in championing women, as it was rare in the early 1900s for women like Judy's grandmother to be educated and literate.

When Judy's father was only 14, his father died. This time it was her grandmother, recently widowed, who used her education and inner strength to hold the family together. She had lived through tumultuous changes and risks during the fall of imperial China, World War II, and famine, and she was determined to make it through this as well. Judy thought about her grandmother and the example she set, and then she knew that she didn't have to choose. She could pursue the purpose buried deep in her heart that was leading her through a risky and winding path. And she could also treasure the tradition that flowed through her veins. Her life might not look traditional, but she didn't have to leave tradition behind.

With her mental barriers shattered, Judy's true purpose was free to emerge and evolve. She focused on self-leadership, intellectual leadership, and risk leadership. For self-leadership, she would identify and pursue global opportunities based on her personal vision. For intellectual leadership, she would continually pioneer new thinking to create value and stay relevant. For risk leadership, she would take personal and financial risks in developing businesses. With that, she cofounded and became the managing director of Dragonfly, providing strategy, quantitative risk management, and investment evaluation for CEOs and boards across all industry sectors worldwide. To pursue her purpose, Judy took substantial personal and financial risk. This was before startups were in vogue, and Judy had no safety net. The safe move would have been to stay with a corporation, but again, she followed her heart. She had an expertise, a vision, and a mission to help leaders analyze risks better and make smarter decisions for themselves and their companies. Her ability to navigate ambiguity, change, and risk is a hallmark of how she helps companies transform and develop strong risk management capabilities and culture.

Judy lives by her mantra that everyone is her teacher and that in observing others she can reflect and constantly improve. She built up her resilience and flexibility. She focused on reinventing herself repeatedly by not fixating on identity and ego. Her business grew along with her reputation as a thought leader in risk management. For 20 years, she continued to identify new opportunities for personal and professional growth. She built another company, Dragonfly Capital, which develops and structures investments in solar, wind, and hydro renewable-energy power plants in Southeast Asia. The company also provides a platform for US-datacenter acquisitions by Asian clients, and develops pipeline and deal structuring for Asian investors entering the US market.

The year 2020 was the 20th anniversary for Dragonfly, which seems ironic given the fact that the global pandemic plunged us into the greatest uncertainty the world faced in a century. It is, however, the perfect time to question everything again. Judy is working with corporations to help them set new visions and rethink strategies, with a deeper understanding that risk is much broader and more linked than what was previously believed. Her experience in working through her own, as well as many leaders' and companies' risks, positions her perfectly to lead others through this time of unprecedented uncertainty to help them choose between paths, and to find purpose in leading organizations for both financial performance and societal benefits. Judy believes that powerful meaning is found in being a part of a greater community, sharing an understanding of people and history, practicing compassion while driving for excellence, being forward thinking and courageous in the face of risks, and knowing that at the end of the day, it's a journey.

Words of Wisdom from Judy to You

- You transform yourself from inside. You make impact by taking action outside.
- In our culture, birthdays are a time when we show gratitude to our parents, because we wouldn't be here without them. I use my birthdays as my annual time for reflection and planning.

- So from a place of gratitude, reflect on why you are here, who you are at the most fundamental level, and then determine what you want to be and how you want to show up.
- It starts with self-awareness. As leaders, we need a quiet space to really think about what motivates us and how to drive forward while replenishing our stores of energy to do what we need to do. It means that we must dig deep inside to refine our ourselves, because who we are inside—what we stand for—is what we bring to the world.
- I practice meditation. It's an important part of my routine. I believe that with the core strength built from self-awareness you can direct your energy and drive with intelligence and heart. Find that space where you get to know who you are, your authentic self. Then you say, okay, with this energy and power, this is what I can do for the world. So, it's an inner stillness, a quiet confidence. Quiet inner time that is followed by concerted purposeful action and output.
- I'm a planner. I will set goals and plan decades into the future. This allows me to take on challenges and do things with a lot of consistency and persistence. Because it's a long-term plan, I won't be fazed by short-term setbacks. In the face of extreme risks and uncertainty, it's an approach that gives you direction, guidance, and markers. You have time to reflect and refine, and refocus as needed, because you are watching how it may all play out. You become more resilient. You are able to create more options, find more opportunities. Your staying power is reinforced, because you can see the big picture, and you're playing the long game.

Chapter 2

Resiliency

"I want you to be everything that's you, deep at the center of your being."

—Confucius

THE FOLLOWING STORIES HAVE AN underlying theme of resiliency, that internal mental fortitude that helps you keep getting up in the face of adversity. Leadership requires a lot of resiliency, and every story in this book is laden with it from beginning to end, but the following stories have a particular level of resiliency that may actually be closer to what the Finnish people call *sisu*, a stoic attitude that "enables individuals to power on when they've reached the end of their psychological or physical resources."[1]

These stories show a depth of will that is, at times, the only thing between success and failure. One of the great things about the human spirit is that we almost always have more inside of us than we know. It's not always the right thing to do, to keep pushing, and you will see that in some of the following stories where this will to continue can cause burn-out, sometimes in the extreme. But there are times when it's necessary, and when you face the need, we know that you will surprise even yourself at the strength you have inside of you.

---

1. Baer, D. (2014, June 17). This Untranslatable Finnish Word Takes Perseverance To A Whole New Level [blog post]. Retrieved January 05, 2021, from https://www .businessinsider.com/finnish-word-sisu-is-key-to-success-2014-6

Bonnie Hagemann

CEO, EDA, Inc.
Location: Kansas City,
Missouri, United States

My Highest Achievements

1. Building a leading human capital firm with a clear and compelling vision to transform the business by designing and building a proprietary, culture-revealing technology platform
2. Becoming a trusted strategic adviser to boards, CEOs and C-suite leaders in large, private and publicly traded companies and because of that she is called upon to speak, advise leaders, write, and inform the media on leadership
3. Creating a life focused on advancing leadership from coaching CEOs to cofounding the WomenExecs on Board network to guiding the young potential leaders across my kitchen table

Stumbling Blocks or Stepping-Stones

Next stop, President. Why not the top?

That's an inscription on the yellow sticky note inside Bonnie's cabinet door. It's from her dad, a Western Oklahoma farmer who had a 142

IQ, a 9th grade education, and very limited exposure to the world but who instinctively knew the importance of helping his children see themselves far beyond the small world they lived in. Bonnie never aspired to be president, but she remembers her dad's encouragement not to define herself by current circumstances. Both of her parents provided support and guidance, daily demonstrating the importance of vision, determination, courage, and hard work.

Growing up on a large family farm instilled in Bonnie the drive to work hard, to love deeply, and care about land, animals, and people. She attended a state university only an hour away from the family farm so she could go home and help if needed. Bonnie's standard mode of operation is to identify a vision or goal, jump in the deep end, and rely on endurance and hard work to figure out what to do when she gets there. With that attitude, she put her head down, worked, and played as hard at college as she did on the farm and completed college in three years.

After a few stepping-stone jobs, Bonnie was recruited by the company that publishes the Myers-Briggs Type Indicator® and other assessments, and led consultative sales in eight states for five years. She loved the job, but with no upward positions likely to open anytime soon, she decided it was time to grow and founded her own human capital firm, in 2001. She had barely launched when the September 11th terrorist attacks in the United States turned her hopes from quick growth to survival. Fortunately, she had a few major clients that helped the company survive the down market, and by 2007 Bonnie was ready to take the company to the next level.

They were providing consulting and leadership development to large companies up to about the vice president level, but remembering her dad's encouragement *Why not the top?* Bonnie was determined to get her company to the top of the house. Given that she did not have a business degree or the time to go back and get one, she hired two business coaches to teach her how to run a business by the numbers, how to raise capital, and how to complete acquisitions.

Eventually she found the perfect target, a company in California called Executive Development Associates, a top-of-the-house custom executive development firm with a high-end brand and a trusted, global reputation for quality design and delivery of executive education to the top 5 percent in the companies they served. She completed the acquisition in January 2007, merged the two companies, and pulled together a strategy team to raise capital for a roll-up of underperforming complimentary companies in the industry when, once again, the blue skies turned ominous, and the storm caused by the subprime mortgage crisis rolled in. EDA's revenue dropped to one-third of expectations, and with the debt from the acquisition, the whole company was upside down and going deeper by the day, eventually hitting bottom with over $1 million in debt, all personally guaranteed.

The lessons Bonnie learned during this time came hard and fast. Leaning on her roots, she decided not to file bankruptcy but to pay back every penny by working however hard and however long it took. She took the staff down to the bare bones and closed both physical offices, moving to a 100 percent virtual environment years before it was a popular thing to do. Most weeks she worked between 70 and 80 hours, only taking breaks to take care of her two children in the evenings before going back to work late into the night. Before it was over, she worked three years without a paycheck and only three days off.

Once in this cycle, she had trouble getting herself out of it and didn't stop until she became so physically sick that she couldn't get out of bed for a week. Her business partner and friend, Annette Klososky, came to the rescue. She pulled everything off Bonnie's plate and over to hers, insisting that she focus on rest and recovery. It took several weeks before she was fully functioning, but eventually Bonnie went back to work and with help from Annette and others figured out how to stop the destructive work cycle.

Even though she wasn't working as many hours, Bonnie was still suffering from serious burnout. All of the joy had left, and each day it took everything inside of her just to get up, put on her game face, and keep going. She would mentally escape by dreaming of being born in an earlier time with a shop that closed around 5:00 p.m. each evening, where she could turn the sign around to *Closed* and wave through the window while she swept the floor. But that was just a dream, and the work never stopped.

She didn't expect to get over the burnout, but step by step and dollar by dollar, she and her team dug the company out of debt, and one day it was as if her heart's power cord was picked up and plugged back in. The light, the joy, and her spark returned. Her passion was as strong as it ever had been, but she was much wiser and maybe a little weathered from the process. The company was 100 percent out of debt and growing with a new technology division in mid-build, when COVID-19 hit.

But this time was different. Having been through two major downturns before, Bonnie knew what to do and how to lead the company through it. She also knew that even if the worst possible scenario happened, the team members would all eventually be okay. This time with greater perspective, Bonnie knew two things: 1. Many companies in her industry will go under; and 2. If they can do a good job getting through this, EDA can emerge in an even better position than they were before, with less competition and greater trust from their clients. She also learned the power of appropriate rest and rarely works more than 60 hours herself and almost never asks for more than 40 hours a week from her highly performing, trusted team, although they freely give more when it is needed.

Today, Bonnie continues to lead EDA, and she has emerged as a sought-after speaker, author, and adviser on leadership issues, and then in an unexpected turn she has become a passionate advocate for gender equality in senior leadership positions and on corporate boards. When she realized the depth of the gender issue, she did what she always does, jumped in the deep end, and started making a path. In that light, she cofounded WomenExecs on Boards and is working to get on a public company board herself so she can have an impact from a governance stance. However, with EDA turning tech, she will be going for the top once again, and if she doesn't get on someone else's public company board, she may just have to build one.

WORDS OF WISDOM FROM BONNIE TO YOU

- It's going to be okay. Don't give up.
- Bring your A-game every day.
- Don't just get a seat at the table, get the power seat.
- When you see a leadership gap, step in it.
- Help as many people as you can along the way.

Owning and Addressing Product Launch Failure

AINSLIE SIMMONDS

Global Head of Digital, PIMCO
Location: Larchmont, New York,
United States

MY HIGHEST ACHIEVEMENTS

1. Built and sold Learnvest ($350 million exit) as COO to Northwestern Mutual
2. Built and sold thinkorswim ($850 million exit) as CPO to TD Ameritrade
3. Building digital group at PIMCO ($2 trillion work in progress) as global asset manager

STUMBLING BLOCKS OR STEPPING-STONES

Ainslie Simmonds will tell you that there was a lot of luck in her two successful dot-com exits, but it's more likely that she is a highly competent and extremely intuitive leader. A person who reported directly to her describes her as "incredibly intelligent, wonderfully straightforward and when she talks, people listen—for good reason, too. Her marketing instincts are killer, her presentation style is compellingly real, and her mentorship has been absolutely instrumental in my career."[1] There may have been a little luck along the way, but Ainslie was prepared.

She was born on the Windsor side of the Detroit, Michigan–Windsor, Ontario border region, which is a hub for trade between Canada and the United States. She spent her formative years in Toronto, attained her bachelor's degree from Ivey Business School at Western University in London, Ontario, earned her MBA from Harvard, and took her first job out of college in Philadelphia, Pennsylvania, at Campbell Soup Company. These experiences were already giving her a broad perspective and helping to develop her intuition about people, cultures, and markets. She had started working in marketing, but as she went through the next two jobs and companies, she made the transition to digital marketing. She had become intrigued with the internet and all things digital, and she decided to make the big leap to the startup world.

The pivot from large-company profit-and-loss economics to startup economics was a bit startling and difficult to adjust to. She was comfortable in her understanding of how to build and grow business from a corporate standpoint, but the startup world was humbling. The models were very different; she had to learn fast, be okay with failure, and admit that the 25-year-olds knew this game better than she did. There were, however, some similarities that she knew well, such as how to be user centric and data driven. As chief marketing and product development officer for her first startup, thinkorswim, a high-frequency options trading platform, she demonstrated these competencies convincingly. She did learn fast, and in a four-and-a-half-year whirlwind of growth, she and her colleagues grew the company from approximately $40 million to several-hundred million, took the company public, and then sold it to TD Ameritrade in an $850 million exit.

Ainslie learned a lot about herself in the process, and one thing was that while she enjoyed marketing, the move into product development and operations increased her passion. She felt that she had much more impact when she could lead teams to build new things versus change and tweak on marketing and branding messages. In subsequent moves, she has been able to stay in these more impactful roles: she has already had another exit of $350 million, with Learnvest and is currently working on her third and biggest opportunity yet, with PIMCO, a company laser-focused on finding and creating opportunities for active, fixed-income investors.

But it hasn't all been one J-Curve after another. In one of her ventures, Ainslie led a new product development that turned into a start-up's worst nightmare. They did all the research on what to build. They invested a significant amount of venture capital. They did all the work to make sure it was a great product. They created best-in-class marketing and did a stellar rollout. And... nothing. No buyers, few inquiries, and little interest. Her team was stunned, and so was she. She had no idea what happened, but doing nothing was obviously not an option. She knew that as a leader she needed to figure out a direction and start moving the team forward.

As an introvert, she needed to think, and she needed to be alone to tear into the problem and figure out what the right question to ask was before she started talking to a lot of others who would undoubtedly point her in a lot of different directions. She went home and spent time sorting out all possible causes. Was it the wrong product or the wrong marketing? No one had an absolute answer, so she had to make a call, and the next decision was the biggest and most difficult of her career. Her intuition said that it wasn't that they had the wrong product but that they weren't marketing it correctly. So she made the call, and they completely retooled the marketing approach. It worked, but as Ainslie thinks back, she knows that it could just have easily not worked.

Ainslie has learned that living in the dot-com world means that you live with a certain level of discomfort, especially if the company is growing fast. She never felt ready for the next step. She and her colleagues just took the steps one by one, because they had to, and tried to figure it out when they got there. She continuously worried that they were taking on more than they could handle, but somehow they kept handling it anyway.

It's a constant stretch, sometimes almost to the breaking point. She now understands that high growth means that things never feel completely manageable and the decisions are rarely clear-cut. If you want clear and manageable, the startup world is probably not the right career path. They live on the edge.

The other big lesson she learned is that great startups are built when you love the problem and not the solution. For example, the problem Ainslie has been trying to solve for 20 years is to help Americans have a better relationship with their wallet, but to do so in a way that also has greater social and business outcomes. She is passionate about this problem, and it keeps her motivated and excited. In the same vein, being in love with the problem is an entrepreneur's superpower. It opens their aperture and gives them a never-ending joy of trying to figure out the problem. Whether they get it right or get it wrong, they are always learning about the problem. It makes for a beautiful career.

Words of Wisdom from Ainslie to You

Be as humble as you can. When the world shifts, you must be willing to go back to the beginning, to be a learner again and to be very aware and somewhat afraid of your own biases. The right way is not the way you learned, but the way that works today. The global pandemic of COVID-19 has shifted our world, and what worked yesterday may not work today. Go back, be humble, and learn all over again.

---

1. Ainslie Simmonds Profile Page. LinkedIn. Retrieved December 13, 2020, from https://www.linkedin.com/in/ainslie-simmonds-10a6b214/

Christine Fellowes

Managing Director, Networks,
APAC at NBCUniversal
Location: Singapore, Asia

My Highest Achievements

1. Led NBCUniversal's Asia Pacific business, launching television networks and driving growth through diversification as the industry transformed digitally
2. Supported pivotal mergers and business integration when Turner Broadcastingwas acquired by Time Warner, and when Comcast Corporation acquired NBCUniversal
3. Served as cochairman of Asian Academy Creative Awards

Stumbling Blocks or Stepping-Stones

Christine is the managing director of NBCUniversal Networks Asia-Pacific, leading the APAC region, as well as the US-based International Media Distribution (IMD) business unit, responsible for their media networks and digital services portfolio. She's impressive by any standards, but the quality that most stands out is her authenticity. For a woman who works in a world that creates dreams and escapism, she is surprisingly grounded and transparent.

Christine grew up in Perth, in Western Australia.

She lived near the ocean, which fostered an enormous love of nature and passion for outdoor adventure. Today Christine hikes in the rainforests, loves ocean swimming and running. Being outdoors keeps Christine grounded in what is real and meaningful and balances the demands of her corporate life.

Before a career in media and entertainment, Christine earned a bachelor's degree in economics from the University of Western Australia (UWA) and worked in Sydney's fashion industry.

While visiting friends in Hong Kong, who were investing in technology and pioneering Asian pay television, she fell in love with the city's intoxicating mix of East and West. It was sophisticated and entrepreneurial, exciting, fast-paced, and a future hub for media and technological development for the region. Christine was inspired by the energy and exhilarating pace, with endless career and business opportunities, so she decided to stay without even returning home from vacation. But first she needed to let her family know her plans.

Running low on funds but fueled by a dream of adventure, Christine called home and asked her mom, Marjorie, for advice. It was not an easy decision and there was risk in making a spontaneous move like this without a backup plan, but Christine believed in herself and felt confident she could develop the opportunities and build a career. Christine's mom didn't hesitate and told her to go for it! She reminded her daughter that life presents choices and will take you where you need to go. She encouraged adventure, urging her daughter to follow her dreams. Christine also spoke to her sister and best friend, Janet who was supportive and loved that she'd have such an exciting place to visit in the future!

Christine stayed in Hong Kong and soon secured a job at Omnicom Media Group developing new business and opening new markets. Christine was not only in love with Hong Kong, she was also in love personally and soon married and started a family. Christine was ambitious, diving into everything that would fast track her knowledge and exposure into the culture and business landscape. With her trademark energy and commitment, she achieved continued success and was rising in her field when the Turner Broadcasting company recruited her, and she transitioned from the agency to the client side of the business. The pressure and demands were rising along with the excitement as her responsibilities increased.

There were not many women leaders in media and entertainment at that time and few female role models. Corporate life was challenging but one-dimensional. Christine was determined to continue to elevate her career but also wanted to be the best mother that she could be. Both were important and required different kinds of energy, but it could be exhausting and lonely for a young mother. Conversation in the office or boardroom with male colleagues was narrow. She never spoke of her home life, a sick child, or anything about her interests outside business.

Today, women have more freedom to bring their whole self to work, but it was different then. She threw herself into strategies for market growth and developed strategic joint ventures and partnerships, which propelled her career and opportunities continued to flourish. She was nine months pregnant with her second child when she received a call for her dream role at the C-suite executive leadership level with E Entertainment, to spearhead their development of Asia.

After multiple interviews she was offered the position and invited to fly to LA to meet the president. She hadn't considered that motherhood would be reason to pause, but she explained that she couldn't get there until after her baby was born.

Her new president understood that she would manage her priorities successfully and assured her of his support. His experience growing up with six accomplished sisters was that women were adept time managers and multitaskers. Christine was finally in a place where it was recognized and appreciated that women (and men) who have family life outside work, were often the most productive, well adjusted, and effective. They were able to perform under pressure with competing priorities in a way that was enormously valuable in business. Her commitment was solidified, and she accepted the new role with great passion and energy.

Invited to attend a major global industry event, called NATPE, hosted every year in Las Vegas, Nevada, Christine knew it would be an intense but exciting opportunity to meet all the senior executives as well as their major international clients. She had to be focused, energized, well prepared.

It also meant she needed to fly across the world with her newborn. She invited her mom to accompany her and help with baby Kiaya. However, when she arrived in the US, the physical and mental stress of the fifteen hour flight with an infant, jet lag, and sleep deprivation, along with the rigorous challenge of industry learning and preparation ahead of an intense packed meeting schedule, started to take its toll.

While trying to do everything perfectly, Christine soon realized that when juggling career and family, perfection was neither realistic nor necessary. Doing well doesn't mean you have to be perfect in everything. Being highly motivated and conscientious is still achievable, but she'd have to drop the all-or-nothing mindset.

Christine wanted to be the best possible mother and was committed to nursing her baby, but she had underestimated the physical pressure of her situation and the inability to set her schedule to accommodate a baby's feeding time. Marjorie watched her daughter juggle time and energies, saw how her increased anxiety was impacting her nursing and sleep. She stepped in and suggested getting baby formula and provided the reassurance Christine needed to make a practical decision for her young infant.

After time to sleep and gain clarity, Christine realized her excessively high standards were unrealistic and unnecessary. She was able to restructure her schedule so she could be more effective in all aspects. Being adaptive and flexible while striving for excellence and knowing when to let go are important considerations when balancing multiple priorities.

She was soon able to get back to the conference and clients. It was a difficult time, and looking back, Christine realized she had to stop, rebalance, and prioritize, to manage a new baby, new job, and new environment all at the same time. What she learned as a mother also applied to leadership. She learned to analyze competing priorities, focus on the most critical with 100 percent of her attention when needed, and ultimately, with the right support and resources, reach a balance that allowed her to move between priorities to achieve the greatest impact.

There have been many extremely challenging times, but none more anxiety producing than having a newborn with a new job and trying to do it all perfectly. She wasn't the perfect mom, but she worked really hard to be the best that she could be, and today, her kids are happy, healthy, and proud of their mom. Christine's most rewarding accomplishment is being close to her three children and watching them develop into extraordinary young adults, and her greatest aspiration is to be as wise and loving as her mom.

WORDS OF WISDOM FROM CHRISTINE TO YOU

To young women whose role as a mother is everything, for whom career is really important—and who feel ambitious and excited by that—I'd say:

- Listen to your intuition (and your mother!); block out the external judgment and internal chatter in your head. You know like no one else what's best for you and your children.
- Families are resilient, and love truly conquers all.
- There is no right way to do things. Forge your own unconventional path and definition of success in everything you do.
- Prioritize ruthlessly and learn when to say no.
- Done is better than Perfect.
- Be brave, and try things. Take risks. You've got this!

EMMANUELLE MACE-DRISKILL

Executive Director of Product and
Strategic Planning at Charles and
Keith Group
Location: Singapore

MY HIGHEST ACHIEVEMENTS

1. Established a goal to change jobs/functions every three to five years, to keep learning about culture. Worked for different multinational companies from UK, France, Italy, US, China, and Singapore. Have lived a very interesting journey requiring a lot of energy to constantly adapt and keep learning while progressing on the corporate ladder.
2. Filled roles at big jobs, including L Capital Asia—LVMH, as regional manager for Marc Jacobs, and executive director with Charles & Keith, developing the brands, from building the brand awareness to distribution. (For Marc, we started with a network of 30 stores, and in four years we opened more than 120 stores becoming one of the leading fashion brands for LVMH.) Raised brand equity and strengthened the fashion culture by partnering with leading designers/stylists and media, fueling our growth for the Chinese market tripling total sales volume, with a total

network of 600 stores and 5,000 employees. It is a family-owned business, and I have been selected to serve on the board.

3. Managed to convince employer to let me open a sustainability department in a location where sustainability has only recently gained traction. Broached this hot topic through difficult conversations to establish a long-term sustainability strategy that's critical to the company. From first conversation, opened the department within two years.

STUMBLING BLOCKS OR STEPPING-STONES

Emmanuelle Mace-Driskill has lived a life of adventure, full of exploration, change, and learning. She was born in Dieppe (Normandy) France, but even as a young girl, she didn't see herself as only French. She saw herself as a part of the global human experience, and she wanted to live and learn all over the world, and she has done just that. She's traveled all over, speaks four languages, and has lived in the United Kingdom, France, Italy, the United States, China, and Singapore. Her experiences have led her to much personal growth and a broad understanding of the world with plenty of excitement, struggles, and the continuous need for adaptation along the way.

Emmanuelle started her journey after high school. She went to the Paris Nanterre University in Nanterre, France, and obtained a BA in German literature and later went on to study at Ecole franco-allemande de Commerce et d'Industrie (EFACI)—French German business school/ Erasmus program, where she got her BA in international trade. From there, she was fortunate to receive an internship in Hong Kong. She was fascinated by the energy of Hong Kong, and Asia offered a whole new world to explore that one could only achieve by living in it.

She was a quick learner and a good leader. Within a short time, she moved into a full-time position with the luxury brand Givenchy, running all the duty-free stores for them. There were mostly men in management, and she was young, so it wasn't easy to find her place, but she was determined to make it.

Despite being a woman, her success made her marketable, and she made a couple of moves and then landed a great job with Marc Jacobs, an American fashion designer.

Her role was in Hong Kong, and she oversaw Asia-Pacific development, which ended up being a great success. Along the way, she married an American citizen, and it was probably an asset when she joined Marc Jacobs, which is part of LVMH group. It was an interchange of cultures with LVMH management in France, and Marc Jacobs management in the US. Fortunately, Emmanuelle's experience in the three cultures helped as the male-dominated French culture met the strong, powerful women on the Marc Jacobs New York management team, and all were trying to do business in Asia. They all felt that she was one of them, and in some ways, she was one of all of them. She understood every side, but it was very political and not very healthy for her in the long run. She wanted to move on, and she wanted to move to Singapore. Fortunately, LVMH didn't want to lose her, and they asked her to help them with another one of their portfolio investments in Singapore, which she accepted and then later moved to her current company Charles & Keith (L'Capital, private equity arm of LVMH, invested in Charles & Keith in 2011 as minority stake holder).

Along the way, there were three major struggles. The first was working with majority men in an Asian environment, where things like getting pregnant seemed like a career death sentence and did hurt her career at the time. Even though Emmanuelle was committed to getting back to a great path and helping pave a way for women coming behind her, she had to put up with all the adjustments of the times. If she spoke up, she was too aggressive. Men would say that she forgot to be a woman, and other distracting and unhelpful comments. Despite this, or maybe because of it, she was thriving, but it wasn't easy.

The second was when LVMH sent her to Charles & Keith, a company rooted in Singapore culture whose aspirations were to become global. The owners challenged her to change the company culture, turn them into a fashion brand, and help them to become a global brand. This was a new experience, because she was used to working with worldwide-established brands, and she underestimated the role of culture in how this would go. She also overestimated the work ethic in Singapore, assuming initially that it would be the same as Hong Kong. She was coming from a corporate western culture where dynamics at work are quite different from a family owned business. The founders created their company at a very young age and she was the first non-Asian female executive in the company. She was given the challenge to transform the company into a global fashion brand which just meant to change the company culture. She was an elephant in the room coming from a very different background and the founders had neither the foundations nor the experience to manage a person like herself and the change she was bringing to the company. The other major problem was that her colleagues in the company fought every improvement, from recruiting new talent to initiating new projects. They either felt threatened or simply did not want to change, but either way, it made her job especially difficult. And that led to her third challenge: burnout.

Despite the culture challenges, Emmanuelle was determined to get Charles & Keith to another level, and they did get to another level; but it came at a high price, and she went into complete burnout. She had to take a full month off to recover. She had lost her balance. She was working too much and was too involved, treating the company as if it were her own. She learned the hard way that leadership is about so much more than results, and it took some outside help to get through it.

She took a couple of Harvard Business School courses that helped her to understand and better analyze and reflect on the meaning of leadership. She learned to be both vulnerable and resilient, which allowed her to become a stronger person and hopefully a smarter leader. She had also hired an incredible and smart young woman, Severine Savignan, who had made a 360-degree change in her life by becoming a yoga instructor and converting to Buddhism. They had become friends, so when she saw Emmanuelle in distress, she came and helped her get through this difficult period. She taught her how to practice yoga and read meditative texts, and these practices helped Emmanuelle take a long pause and begin a season of self-reflection. She found yoga to be like soft medicine to the body, just paying attention to breathing and state of mind and letting both her mind and her body recover from the years of overworking. Over time, she began to clear her mind and rebalance. Having a close friend like Severine and an incredibly supportive husband were lifesavers during this time. She and her husband went for regular retreats in Bali and Cambodia, taking the time to put down the world's cares and embrace their vulnerable state of being human, to relax, to read and to reflect.

Through this experience, Emmanuelle has come to a new level of enlightenment, and she thinks a lot about all the things she's learned. She believes that we need to reshape the world, both for the sake of the planet and for the sake of our human condition. So many people are becoming lost in the work, the need to make more money, to win and to get more information through technology. As humans, we're so much more than that, and perhaps we are losing the art of being human, of just being and making sense of the world. She lost it personally for a while, but through the experience of burnout and recovery, she gained something, a new self-awareness, a new balance, a new life.

Words of Wisdom from Emmanuelle to You

- Learn to say no. Know your own limits, and dare to speak up.
- Project yourself where you want to be in next five to 10 years. It helps you to set your priorities.
- Start early, and be diligent about building your network.
- Spend more time networking and less time trying to be perfect.
- Get mental support.
- Know where your values are.
- Education is key.
- Be curious always and have an open mind. Have an appetite for life. You have so much to learn, so keep learning.

Rebecca (Riv) Goldman

SVP and General Council, Optimas
Solutions
Location: Milwaukee, Wisconsin,
United States

My Highest Achievements

1. Winning an unwinnable case in federal court in her second year of law school, achieving full inclusion for a child with autism
2. Moving from paralegal—as a yet-unlicensed lawyer—to general counsel of a General Electric (GE) business, in seven years
3. Mentoring hundreds of women from the US and across the globe in multiple corporations as they work their way up the corporate ladder

Stumbling Blocks or Stepping-Stones

There's a picture of a woman as she finishes her first Sprint Triathlon, a multisport event that consists of a 750m swim, a 20k bike, and a 5k run. Her hands are in the air, and there is blood running down her arm after a painful fall during the biking portion of the race. That picture is of Riv Goldman, and it tells you everything you need to know about Riv. She sets her eyes on the target and makes a plan, and no matter how many obstacles are in the way or how painful the path, she keeps getting up and pursuing the goal. She is mentally tough, stubborn, witty, and loving all at the same time.

Today, Riv is SVP and General Counsel of Optimas OE Solutions, a specialty distributor and manufacturer of highly engineered fasteners and components, headquartered in Glenview, Illinois, United States. It's owned by private equity and just under a billion dollars in sales. She is also serving on a private company board and is involved in several nonprofit activities relating to services for children and adults with disabilities.

Initially, Riv prepared herself for the business world by completing a bachelor's degree in economics from Stanford University and an MBA from the Kellogg School of Management at Northwestern University. Her career jumped into high speed as she secured a position in a financial management training program for Johnson & Johnson, in their McNeil Consumer Products Division. McNeil had just hired a new CEO from Procter & Gamble, charged with taking this little-known over-the-counter product—Tylenol—from behind the pharmacy counter to mega status. It was exciting and unconventional at the same time.

The work was fun and exciting for a newly minted MBA, but soon the excitement turned into crisis management, as Riv was chosen to be a part of the response team for a 1982 series of poisonings involving Tylenol that had been laced with potassium cyanide, widely known as the Chicago Tylenol Murders. Although the perpetrator was not identified, Johnson & Johnson/McNeil have long been recognized for taking a customer-centric approach to handling this crisis. Capsules were replaced with tablets and those choosing Tylenol were given a safe alternative to use.

At 23, Riv found that she excelled in this environment and was soon catching her boss's attention as a rising star. He told her she could be running a business at Johnson & Johnson (J&J) in a relatively short period of time, but even as her head was filled with hope for an exciting future, Riv found herself facing a difficult decision. She also had a new husband, and he had a family business in his hometown of Springfield, Illinois.

The business needed him, so one of them had to sacrifice, and like many women in the business world at that time, Riv took a deep breath and made the decision to go where her husband's work needed him.

Springfield was a major transition into a world that wasn't the life she had dreamed of, but Riv didn't let her new circumstances get her down. She soon went to work in Springfield for a multiline insurance company. Ever the optimist, Riv found this work fun as well. She did annual budgeting and financial planning. Later she expanded her understanding of various parts of the business by moving into marketing, where she learned to conduct focus groups, direct mail, and more. All was going well when her husband's family decided to sell the business. Riv was relieved to exit Springfield, although their time there did have silver linings, as they now had two children.

Riv shined up her résumé and started applying for work elsewhere. She soon landed a position with turnaround opportunity at an insurance company in Springfield, Ohio, and this time her husband moved for her work and found a position in their new city.

This company offered both credit and mortgage insurance. Riv was hired as Vice President of Strategic Planning, and she primarily managed the mortgage part of the business. The company had problems, but she along with others in the company were able to turn the business around and put it on the block to sell.

During the due diligence phase, the acquirers at Ryan Insurance were asking a lot of questions. Not one to skirt the truth, Riv gave them the answers. She felt that the CEO of her company did not appreciate her candor. He was extremely upset. However, he lived in Chicago, and Riv knew that he wouldn't fire her over the phone, so she just had to make sure they were never in the same place at the same time. She felt like she was dodging a subpoena, but it worked, and she managed to dodge him long enough for the new owners to realize a few important facts. Ultimately, he moved on and Riv was offered a position at Ryan Insurance.

Riv and her husband now both had jobs they liked, but fate threw another obstacle in her path, as they learned that her son Michael had classic autism. Today, we understand autism better, but back then many autistic children were institutionalized. There was a general belief that, cognitively, they wouldn't make it past the third grade, but Riv knew her son, and she didn't believe that third grade would be his stopping place.

She researched the best way to educate a young child with classic autism, and the answer that resonated with her was full inclusion in a regular classroom where support is brought to the child. The only problem was, the school that her son attended didn't see it the same way and tried to put him on a special education track where he would rarely interact with the mainstream children. Riv went to the superintendent and suggested getting the school personnel trained, and even offered to pay for their training so her son could get the support he needed.

The superintendent said no, but Riv didn't give up. She kept researching and found out that the law provides that he can be sitting in the regular classroom, so Riv hired a lawyer to fight for her son. The lawyer ultimately said that she couldn't win the case. Maybe that lawyer couldn't win it, but that didn't mean the case couldn't be won.

Riv decided to do it herself. She turned down the job at Ryan Insurance, started law school, and filed a suit against the school district. The worst part of this experience was not the need to fight for her child; instead, it was standing in federal district court and facing other lawyers and experts who were arguing about the capability of her son. The results were worth the pain, and at the end of her second year of law school, she had won her first case, *Michael W. Goldman v. Centerville School District*. The year was 1993. The court was Federal District Court, Dayton, Ohio.

With the judgment in hand so Michael could attend regular class, Riv decided they needed to find a different, more supportive school district and to find a city where she could finish law school. They found just the place outside of Cincinnati, so they made the move. When Riv finished law school, she needed a job with flexibility so she could be available for Michael when he came home from school at 2:20 p.m., and in case something went wrong at school.

Although well below her skill level by this point, Riv ended up taking a paralegal position at General Electric, often known as GE, in the

Aircraft Engines division. Once again, she took a deep breath, because despite her prestigious degrees, she would only be paid $13 an hour. It was hard, but in her heart she knew it would somehow work out. And it did. She soon passed the bar and renegotiated with her boss to be outside counsel, which allowed her to make much more appropriate wages, to have the flexibility she needed for Michael, and to learn from some of the best in the world, the lawyers at GE. They were doing acquisitions and divestitures all over the world, and Riv was right in the middle of it. It was the perfect complement to everything that she had done up to this point.

Michael ultimately had a very successful high school career and became more independent, freeing Riv up to take a full-time position again, which she did, this time as general counsel for one of GE's business lines. The new role was great, but there were also problems in the business, and in time it was merged with another business unit, so Riv decided it was time to leave.

Her next job, at Rockwell Automation in Milwaukee, also incorporated everything she had learned up to this point, and she enjoyed the work for 10 years before deciding to retire and focus on board roles. As you get the picture of Riv's personality, you can imagine that retirement didn't really fit, and when a former GE colleague took the CEO position at Optimas Solutions and asked Riv to join her team, Riv accepted and today continues to thrive at work while simultaneously establishing a first-of-its-kind intentional community—of 24 autistic adults and graduate students—where Michael and 23 others can thrive.

WORDS OF WISDOM FROM RIV TO YOU

- I'll share with you some advice that my mother gave to me. If you get knocked down or if you take a detour, you're going to come back. Just put one foot in front of the other, and keep moving in the direction of your goal. Even if you're stuck in a particular juncture or there is a mountain in front of you, just keep moving forward.

- Personally, I believe that work also needs to be fun. So, go ahead and take some risks. Know what your value is, and trust that it is all going to work out okay. If you've been successful in one place, then you already know how to do it, and you will find your way to success again. Have a little faith, and like my mother said, keep putting one foot in front of the other. Just keep going.

Joanna Dodd Massey, PhD

President and CEO, JDMA, Inc.
Location: New York, New York,
United States

My Highest Achievements

1. Becoming the senior vice president of communications at one of only six broadcast television networks in the United States at the age of 32, which included overseeing a bicoastal staff and a multimillion-dollar P&L while reporting to the CEO of the company
2. Attaining both a PhD in psychology and an MBA mid-career, while working
3. Authoring two books, *Communicating During a Crisis: Influencing Others When the Stakes Are High* and *Culture Shock: Surviving Five Generations in One Workplace*

Stumbling Blocks or Stepping-Stones

It's no surprise that Joanna Dodd Massey made quick work of the corporate ladder after entering the media industry. Her lively personality, along with her ability to communicate and lead, are second only to her ambition and work ethic. By age 28, she was reporting to CEOs, and by age 32, she had made it to the executive level at major media companies, including CBS, Viacom, Lionsgate, and Condé Nast. Joanna worked in Hollywood and later in New York in one of the most cutthroat industries and cultures.

When you see Joanna, the first thing you will likely notice is that she is attractive, well dressed, and well spoken. You might think this gives her a step up, but being a woman who is also attractive in the business world can be just as much of an obstacle as an advantage. It was often an obstacle for Joanna.

First, there was the gossip that she was achieving her success by sleeping with various C-level men. In order to combat the gossip and to compete with her male colleagues, Joanna worked harder, often two and three times as hard as her male counterparts, only to make less and get backstabbed by female colleagues who were in competition with her for top jobs. Her competitive nature and hard work ethic also took a toll on her personal life and, she concedes, likely contributed to the breakup of her marriage.

Joanna's ambition drove from somewhere deep inside. She couldn't turn it off even if she wanted to, but she didn't want to. She wanted to succeed, and at that time, for a woman to be successful she had to be able to hang out with the guys. There were very few women in the highest-level corporate seats, and those who were had made some adjustments to get there. Women were taught to dress in dark clothing, wear their hair short, and other things that made them fit better in a man's world.

Joanna made the adjustments that were required in her industry. Hanging out with the men at the time meant a lot of things that had nothing to do with Joanna's ability to do the job. It meant schmoozing over drinks and cigars, going with clients and colleagues to strip joints, and other things that she would never consider doing today and would be considered totally inappropriate, but at the time that is how business was done in her industry. Joanna did what she needed to do to be competitive and successful, but the rumors of her success being tied to sleeping with men who were senior to her were the ones that hurt the most.

Joanna didn't need to sleep with someone to get to the top. Her skills, intelligence, and creativity were more than enough, but her outgoing personality and fearless drive to start a conversation with anyone—no matter how powerful—often landed her in situations where she was hit on by men in high positions.

Joanna, like most women during the '90s, had to learn the art of turning down a man in power without offending them. This is not an easy task, even for someone as skilled at communicating as Joanna. She also had to face her own self-scrutiny, often asking herself if she brought this on by her competitive nature, hanging out with the guys, and every other thing she had ever done that could potentially give an entry point for gossip to start.

There wasn't anyone to turn to inside the companies where she worked. This just wasn't a time when women went to Human Resources (HR) if someone abused their power and behaved inappropriately. If she had, it is not likely that she would have been taken seriously or that anything would have been done about it, other than her own job being put in jeopardy. Today it is better for men and women who are treated inappropriately at work, but those were not tools that were available at the time.

Dealing with the men was one thing, but the women, not to be outdone, were often fierce and biting competitors. Many made it hard to be successful, but not all of the women around Joanna were like that. There were also the ones who were true friends. They were the ones that Joanna could call upon to have a glass of wine at the end of a difficult day and share the triumphs and the horrors of her world. And when times were hard, they were her lifesavers.

One woman who greatly helped Joanna was Dawn Ostroff, who is currently the chief content officer at Spotify. Joanna worked for Dawn more than once, and very early on there was a phone call Joanna needed to make. She didn't want to make it, because she just knew they were going to say no. She was in Dawn's office when Dawn asked if Joanna had called a specific person who could help. Joanna had not called, so Dawn encouraged her by reminding Joanna that the worst thing that person could say is no. Joanna reminded her that this was Hollywood and that they were not just going to say no, they were going to say no with gusto and a lot of swear words around it. Dawn said it was still just a no and that she should pick up the phone, make the phone call. That was a good lesson.

Earning her executive stripes in Hollywood was a tough road, but she made it up the ranks quickly, and as she was getting toward the top of the corporate ladder, she assumed that things would get easier. But the most difficult road was yet to come, because in 2006 she started the first of a series of corporate layoffs. In the following 12 years, she was downsized five times. It wasn't logical, and it wasn't fair, but it was reality. If there were two people for one job in a merger, the job went to her male counterpart. Time and again, Joanna faced an unintended career change, but she did not allow herself the luxury of self-pity. She immediately went into action and figured out her next pivot.

Knowing she wasn't alone helped, and she often reached out to both friends and mentors to help her through. One of the most influential cheerleaders in her life was her friend Jennifer. Jennifer encouraged Joanna to take advantage of her circumstances, wherever they led. After one of the successive layoffs, Jennifer told her that if God shuts one door, He will open another, and that if Joanna was stuck hanging out in the hallway waiting for the other door to open, she should just decorate the hallway. And that's what Joanna did: she took advantage of the hallway time and reinvented herself time and again. She even learned how to turn her adversity into a humorous and inspirational teaching tool. She dubbed herself the Queen of Pivoting, and she has turned distress into success with a career path she could not have foreseen. In that 12 years, Joanna has launched her own communications and marketing firm, attained four graduate degrees, including an MBA from the University of Southern California and a PhD from Sofia University, published two books, and shared her experience during lively keynote talks at Fortune 500 companies, trade organizations, and networking groups.

Joanna took each setback as an opportunity, and she also committed to another one of Jennifer's mantras of radical acceptance and total surrender to life as it is. She chose to stop resisting life's everchanging waters and go with the flow. Today, she often helps others do the same as a mentor to many women in business, and as a public and private company board director, a corporate speaker, an author, and a professor at Columbia University.

Words of Wisdom from Joanna to You

- Don't resist reality, because it's a losing battle. Instead, try to enjoy the roller coaster ride of life with all its ups and downs, because the gift of life is the experiences we have here, not the cash and prizes.
- I look at everything in business through the lens of psychology, and resisting what is happening only causes more suffering. So I hope that you will consider adopting the mantra that helps me see a situation clearly and get into action: radical acceptance and total surrender to life as it is.

Make Your Own Rules
to Avoid Burnout

ANNABELLE VULTEE

Executive, EdTech and Digital
Transformation
Location: Zug, Switzerland

MY HIGHEST ACHIEVEMENTS

1. Leading an organization of over 4,000 full-time employees across China, Russia, Indonesia, and Spain
2. Most proud of becoming a genuine leader; finally finding a way to lead publicly but comfortably as an introvert, while still being able to connect with teams on both personal and professional levels

STUMBLING BLOCKS OR STEPPING-STONES

As Annabelle spends her days trekking the Swiss mountains during a reprieve of only three or four advising gigs at a time, she is contemplating her next move. There is a pretty good chance it is going to be something big, as her international leadership of the China business unit for one of the world's largest privately held education companies has given her both the experience and the recognition needed to receive some interesting offers for both board and executive roles.

She is young for the success she has had, and if we were analyzing global talent we might say that she has a long runway, meaning that she likely has many more years of leadership left in her. In fact, as you look at the results and listen to the experiences that she has already had, it is easy to envision Annabelle ringing the stock exchange bell in New York as CEO of a Fortune 500 company. Her demeanor is sincere, and her mindset is strategic, and it is obvious that she doesn't do anything halfway.

Early in her career Annabelle made quick work of the corporate ladder, making two upward moves in under four years at Coca-Cola Company. This was a great entry into the corporate world, and she learned a lot, but she knew there was more that she wanted to do and that there were some things she would need to learn to do it, so she went back to school to get an MBA from Harvard University, followed by a short jaunt through entrepreneurship with her own Mexican restaurant. This adventure lasted less than two years and is what Annabelle would call an early failure but certainly a learning experience with lessons that last even in her work today.

A little humbled by the entrepreneurial quest, Annabelle used her network to get back into a larger corporation, and she was soon running operations in the aviation industry. It was good but not perfect, because the industry just did not get her heart. It did help her realize what she really cared about, and Annabelle decided that her next job needed to include working for a company that had these three things:

1. Internationally minded
2. For profit and
3. Makes people's lives better.

EdTech fit the criteria when Annabelle made a move to EF Education First, one of the world's largest private education companies with a mission to open the world through education. It was a fascinating company with 13 different divisions, in multiple countries, and over 45,000 full-time employees; and it met her criteria. This was it, and Annabelle's career began to soar.

Gaining the trust of the CEO and the founder early on; Annabelle was tapped to go to India, where her straightforward advice to close the division raised her profile, landing her a division president role in the US. After a mere two and a half years running EF's domestic student travel division, she was again asked to take on an internal turnaround of one of EF's largest businesses, based in China. The news came in a memorable way as she returned from a board meeting and was immediately summoned to the CEO's office. Unsure of the meeting's content, she asked if she should prepare anything or bring anything to the meeting. "Chopsticks," was his reply, and then she knew. She was moving to China.

The next seven and a half years turned into the kind of work that Harvard case studies are made from. Annabelle loved the work in the largest business environment in the world. The pace was warp speed, and the competition was fierce. There were nuances to learn, including how to engage with government relations and public relations, and the fact that relationships come first in China. People are loyal to each other, not to companies, and she would have to gain the trust of her employees and colleagues to be successful. She did gain their trust, despite a gaping language barrier. Many of the employees did not speak English, and Annabelle did not speak Mandarin, but she found a way.

She grew the organization by hundreds of millions in annual revenue, led over 4,000 full-time employees across China, Russia, Indonesia, and Spain, added new customers, and turned it into a profitable business. In addition to new markets, she took the lead on product development and growing a nascent digital-only platform, which are now critical to the business.

Because of the demands of trying to be a reasonably good mom, and the 24-hour, fast-paced work environment, Annabelle eventually started to wear down. There were many days when she did not have the time to prep for any discussions on the agenda, because she had to go from one meeting directly to another for weeks on end. Then she would have to travel, and there were dinners and drinks, and on and on. As an introvert, Annabelle needed time to rejuvenate and get her energy back, but there wasn't any, for months on end. Looking back, she says it almost killed her. But she was leading a successful organization, and she knew that she would soon want to secure a successor and move on to new things, so she could see the light at the end of the tunnel. That was 2017.

But while looking for a successor for over a year, the market hit a tipping point. An influx of private-equity investments backing competitors ran up costs of acquisition, a glut of new competing outlets saturated the market, and the overall need versus desire to learn English as an adult shifted in terms of motivation and willingness to pay, as low-end entrances took hold with apps. She had already been ready to leave, but she knew two things: She wouldn't be a good leader if she left now without the right person ready and able to take the reins, and she would learn more through this experience than any of her past experiences. So, she stayed, but her level of fatigue was growing and starting to impact her health. She was moving from exhaustion to burnout. She no longer looked forward to Monday morning. Her skin changed. She began to lose her hair, and she had stomach problems that were bad enough to visit a Chinese-medicine doctor who put her under a contraption that she was pretty sure could have been in a torture chamber. With not much left to lose, Annabelle decided she needed to manage the business and her own life with the same level of commitment.

The first thing she had to do was take control of her time. She stopped letting anyone put anything on her calendar without approval. She assigned her administrative assistant to gently block unexpected visitors to her office so that she could meet with each person on her own terms. And then, in a stroke of genius, she identified an extroverted proxy.

She knew that she only had so much of herself to give, especially now that burnout was taking its toll physically. So she went to one of her talented, extroverted colleagues and said she needed her to join Annabelle on her business trips; and when she couldn't give any more, she needed her colleague to take over. She trusted her colleague to do a good job of speaking on her behalf. She also knew that she would take care of the employees, customers, and other important relationships when Annabelle didn't have it in herself. It worked. Annabelle had made enough space in her life to get through to a meaningful exit. With her proxy and her team rallied around her, she was able to keep leading. And when she did leave, she left well.

She wanted to do the best job she could do in the leadership transition, so she focused on product development and creating a business model for the future. She wanted the next leader to feel 100 percent supported and to give him every piece of knowledge she had, introduce him to every person he needed to meet, and set him up so that he would be successful and able to take care of the people who were working there, as well as the customers. And she did just that. The transition lasted from late 2019 to March 2020, amid COVID-19.

Annabelle and her family had already decided that Switzerland was their next destination, and once borders started opening again, they moved to Zug. This isn't the "travel-the-world-and-smell-the-roses" respite Annabelle had in mind with worldwide COVID-19 restrictions and general concern for exposure, but over the course of three months she has done the interior design of her home, been on Swiss TV, continues to advise two startups, advises private equity firms, and hikes up to 100km a week. It will not be too long before she is ready for her next full-time work adventure, but she is in no rush. The global pandemic has some silver linings for Annabelle, and she intends to treasure every one of them; she strongly believes we need to make our own rules about success, and she is living some of them now.

WORDS OF WISDOM FROM ANNABELLE TO YOU

- First, every leader goes through difficult periods, but all good times come to an end, and all bad times come to an end. Sometimes, people feel like when they are in a really bad rut or really challenging time that this will never end. So ride the highs, and be patient through the lows. You will get through both. They will come to an end, and then you are better for it. You are always better for it.

- As an organizational leader, when times get really tough, you have to take a conscious and aggressive approach to protecting and insulating your people from fear, panic, and the unknown. Overcommunicate, be consistent, and follow through. That gains trust in tough times, even if results are slower to follow, and even if there is a lot of external uncertainty. They need to know what is going on and what you are doing to fix it. Do not sugarcoat what needs to be shared. They need you to be calm, proactive, and in alignment with the overall direction of the organization.

- Nobody knows everything. Remain open and welcoming to others' input and ideas, but be prepared to make a clear decision yourself and to own it. Of course you make better decisions when you are better informed and hear different perspectives. Almost equally important, you build buy-in for the execution phase, which is 100 percent of the results.

- Finally, be yourself. Being true to your strengths, your flaws, and all the nuances that make you unique is the most transformative thing you can do as a leader, and likely the hardest. It is okay to be an introvert, a direct and sometimes combative woman, a mom, a hard-ass, an analytical thinker, a jokester, a dreamer, and a yoga-pants-on-the-weekends regular chick who just loves to work. The hardest part is really loving who you are, not caring what other people think, and living 100 percent with conviction and no apologies. But damn, it is amazing to watch all the pieces of the puzzle fall into place when you fully embrace yourself and show it to the world.

Chapter 3

Adaptability

"Diversity is the one thing we all have in common. Celebrate it every day."

—Anonymous

T HE FOLLOWING STORIES HAVE AN underlying theme of adaptability, the practice of accepting and adjusting to changes in the environment. Adaptability is not change for the sake of change. Instead, it involves effective, purposeful change in response to new information or insights.

Adaptive performance can be reactive or proactive and can result from a change in the environment or your own enhanced understanding of the situation. It can occur at the individual and organizational levels. For individuals, adaptive performance can entail changes to thoughts, beliefs, attitudes, and behaviors. For leaders, adaptive performance entails not only change to self but also developing the adaptive capabilities of others, establishing a climate conducive to adaptive performance, and leading change efforts.

In the stories ahead, you will read about leaders who had to adapt either moderately or monumentally to the shifting environment. Some of the stories in this section have to do with women who were discriminated against based on gender. You will notice that most of the women adjusted to fit in to the men's world they were in.

Today it's different, and women are more and more able to bring their whole selves to work, to dress like women, and to come out of the closet as mothers, wives, partners, daughters, and friends. In other words, today, women can be like women instead of acting like men to fit in, but the stories you will read here occurred as these women were making their way, and it is because of these women and others like them all over the world that women today no longer have to make the same adjustments. In that vein, as hard as some of the stories in this section are to read, the women who went before us paid an even heavier price, and for them, we take a moment to offer our greatest respect and gratitude.

Making Your Voice Heard Over Culture Shock and Discrimination

SHING PAN

Vice President of Marketing and Business Development for Speech Morphing, Inc.
Location: San Francisco, California, United States

MY HIGHEST ACHIEVEMENTS

1. Established myself as a proud intrapreneur early in career. Took risks, though young and inexperienced (but brave, technology-aware, with a sharp sense about market). Leveraged emerging technology and trends to lead initiative on opportunity I spotted and seized on for then-billion-dollar company Silicon Graphics (SGI) to enter a large market they had missed earlier to major competitors. Succeeded in recruiting and onboarding all top application partners in this field, built from ground zero to revenue and entered the market competitively.

2. Becoming an entrepreneur. Cofounded a high-tech startup, taking it from product prototype and definition to an award-winning product and revenue. Led the investment effort; identified and presented to corporate and venture firms, and successfully

secured investments during the economic downturn, Later our
company was acquired. Persevered through obstacles encountered as a female entrepreneur.

3. As one of a few female executives in a male-dominated technology company, managed product marketing for over 7 products. Proud of what I could do but sad about the lack of females
in higher ranks, made a strong effort to support and motivate
women in tech and women in business.

STUMBLING BLOCKS OR STEPPING-STONES

Shing Pan is a passionate, visionary tech leader with an eye for spotting
emerging technology and trends. Her passion and vision showed up
early in her youth in Shanghai, China. One of her early loves was watching James Bond movies. She would watch and dream of her future and
decided that the marine biologist had the best job in the movie, so she
thought that would be a good career. If not, she thought being a jour-
nalist would be another good option, as she loved to write. She did not
become either but was selected to study mechanical engineering at China
Textile University.

She didn't enjoy it at first until she encountered computer-aided
design (CAD) and automation during her limited computer lab hours. It
was in the early days of CAD and simulation, but she was fascinated by
it and wanted to learn more. She also felt the life she was going toward in
China was too predictable for her adventurous spirit. She could see it all
before her: She would sit in her office doing work, have a cup of tea, and
go home, and this would go on day after day. She would work until she
was about 55, and she could already estimate her total earnings. That was
just too predictable. She wanted a different life and was soon on her way
to the US, where she attended Northern Illinois University on a scholar-
ship and obtained an MS in mechanical engineering and later an MBA
from Cornell University.

Still learning the culture in the United States, she went to work as an automation and robotics application engineer for a subsidiary of Emerson Electric company in Chicago, Illinois. She worked hard and was doing well. After a couple of years on the job, she was recruited to Borg-Warner Automotive Research and Development Center as a senior R&D engineer. She had been there only two weeks, when all the senior people that she interviewed with and was looking forward to learning from were let go. Shing was shocked, because in China that is not what happens. You join a company, work hard, pay respect to the elders, get promoted accordingly, and stay in the job the rest of your work life...at least that was the case then. She felt very guilty and cried at her desk, because she thought that somehow they all lost their jobs because a cheaper workforce, like her, joined the company.

It wasn't her fault, of course, but it did shake her out of an assumption that she had about jobs in America. She, and everyone else, is vulnerable. Anyone can be let go. She realized that she needed to get a lot more strategic about her career. So instead of focusing on just her job, she began to pay attention to the industry she was in. She wanted to grasp the whole picture and how what she did contributed, so that she could become better positioned in the industry and not just for her job. Her mindset had also started to shift from working for a specific company for life to working in an industry where the company is simply a stop of your career journey.

Shing loved automotive engineering, but after a few years she felt a little pigeonholed and wanted to pursue something more, which was when she left to pursue her MBA from Cornell. She loved her time there and learning from both her professors and classmates, who came from diverse backgrounds and cultures and brought different viewpoints and perspectives. Her mind opened further. When she completed her MBA, she was ready to make a move.

As she completed her studies, the dot-com world was a hot market, and she received many offers before she graduated. She stayed close to the engineering work when she accepted a job at Silicon Graphics in San Francisco, California. In another culture shock, on her first day she showed up at 7:30 a.m., in her suit and heels, at her new company, where she had to wait outside for a long time until someone showed up. When they finally did, they were quite casually dressed. It took her a good two years to make the adjustment both mentally and in wardrobe, but eventually she settled into California casual. The culture can be deceiving, because they don't start early and they dress casually, but they do work hard, especially in the tech world, where competition is fast and plentiful. This is where Shing excelled. She has always been a hard worker and forward thinking.

Shing transitioned through Silicon Valley in multiple roles internally and externally as she spent a few years on startups of her own. Another culture surprise came after she left Silicon Graphics and realized she was often the only woman in the room in the startup culture. In a few years she would pick up Sheryl Sandberg's book *Lean In* and realize she wasn't the only one dealing with the male-dominated culture. She would read it and feel understood, but that was down the road. At that moment, she felt isolated and frustrated.

She wanted a formal female mentor even if she had to pay, but she couldn't easily find one. Despite being highly educated and very competent and confident, she found that she had to work harder than her male counterparts. She is also a petite, five-foot, three-inch Asian woman with a soft-spoken manner, which didn't help, and she wasn't willing to do what she saw some women do to make it, such as dress like a man to be taken seriously, speak louder to be heard, or sacrifice her personal and family life to climb the corporate ladder. As a woman in the tech culture, she has been humiliated, harassed, ridiculed, discounted, disrespected, cut off, discriminated against, spoken to with abusive language, and more. It has been lonely and at times painful, and it's been the hardest thing she's had to overcome.

Still, Shing has found her way. She has persevered, worked hard, and held her head high. And from Shanghai, to San Francisco, she has always been one to take the road less traveled. She has navigated sometimes treacherous waters to make it to a high-level position as a woman in tech. She made a lot of sacrifices, but she never compromised being a woman, a mother, or a wife, and she's thankful for the help that she's had, including a supportive husband who values women's equality and takes an equal share of child-rearing and household responsibilities. She is now mentoring young women in tech. She has also changed her definition of *mentor* to be broader than a formal relationship and has found that when she looks at it that way, they are all around her. And despite the discrimination she's encountered, she has also found numerous male managers and executives who have valued her contribution and helped with her career along the way.

Words of Wisdom from Shing to You

- You may work for a company, but you should position yourself in an industry. The industry or the market is your playing field.
- Don't stay too comfortable. Be a risk taker, keep learning and innovating/expanding yourself, treat your role as a business, and think beyond the tasks.
- Finally, believe in yourself, and persevere.

Lisa Pent

Client Partner and Head of Diversity &
Inclusion, Capital Markets, Cognizant
Location: New York, New York,
United States

My Highest Achievements

1. Financing my own private college education through hard work
2. Completing a financing to restore a closed paper mill in upstate New York that restored 70 well-paying jobs to a rural community
3. Not being afraid to change career direction, banking to information services to professional services

Stumbling Blocks or Stepping-Stones

Lisa Pent will tell you she grew up in Los Angeles, California, but that's really a short answer to a long story, as she and her family moved 21 times by Lisa's 18th birthday. But they did live in LA the longest, and she was there last before moving to the East Coast. She is one of four children. Her mother worked in the home, waiting to go to the workforce until Lisa and her three siblings were grown; her father sold equipment to banks. He was a successful salesperson, and he was proud of his work.

When he saw a bank on a family vacation, he would gather the family and have them pose in front of the drive-thru delivery systems, so their family albums are highlighted with banks. Whether he meant to or not, Lisa's dad was, at least subliminally, influencing his oldest daughter.

Lisa is naturally both decisive and pragmatic. As she watched her father's success and passion for the banking business, she decided she too wanted to be in the industry, but not in the same way. Even though she was still in high school, she decided that Wall Street was her goal. To have the best chance of success, Lisa felt that she needed to move to the East Coast, so she applied to universities in the East and ended up at Georgetown University, in Washington, DC.

Lisa put herself through college as a bank teller. She didn't get to do the fun activities that many other students enjoyed, but she was building a career, and that was okay for her, because she was focused on being successful. That was her driver from that day to this one, and she was just as determined after college as she was after high school. After graduation, Lisa went to New York, slept on a friend's couch, and started applying with the firms on Wall Street. She soon had a job offer at Merrill Lynch, which she excitedly accepted and went back to DC to pack her bags and move to New York City.

She had two pantsuits, so she put on the best one and reported in for her first day. Thinking she would get to work doing something interesting right away, she was taken aback when she was promptly told that women weren't allowed to wear pantsuits, and then she was sent home to dress more appropriately. In dismay, Lisa left and went shopping to find a suit with a skirt and then realized, she would need five. This was Lisa's first encounter with what has turned out to be a career full of gender discrimination and male-dominated behavior. This was the mid-1980s, and the firms looked like today's movie sets with men walking around and smoking cigars. The finance world, and especially Wall Street, was and to a great extent still is male dominated, with women making up only 24 percent of Wall Street's ranks as recently as 2019, a number that is lower than the previous decade, when women were at 26 percent, in 2010.[1]

Lisa's first day was rough and a letdown for a recent grad eager to get to work for a company she admired. Fortunately, Lisa isn't easily defeated. She bought the expected clothing and went to work. She did well, achieved results, and began to move up the corporate ladder, progressing from Analyst to Associate to Vice President and then Senior Vice President, but along the way there was gender discrimination. Lisa changed companies several times, but the culture on Wall Street at that time was competitive, with some level of arrogance and misogyny, and Lisa had to fight feeling negative about it. She would walk out of her door on some days feeling fantastic and ready to tackle the world, only to encounter demeaning behavior by her colleagues at work. She would begin to question herself, and her energy would drop. It was challenging and emotionally draining on many days, and shocking on other days.

In one of the more shocking instances, Lisa remembers waking up at 4:00 a.m. to get on a plane and fly to a client site. She spent eight hours with the client and then took another plane back to New York. Her boss insisted that she return to the office. When she arrived, it was around 10:00 p.m. He told her that he needed her to stay at work all night to run the numbers for the client. Since Lisa had spent the day with the client, she knew that the numbers were not needed the next day, but her boss insisted. So, Lisa stayed. At that time, there weren't a lot of personal computers, so Lisa went into the computer room to work. There were already others in the room, mostly men, and they were looking at pornography. They didn't even bother to put the magazines away when she came in or when other higher-level leaders did.

In another company, Lisa was on the holiday party planning committee. The company always gave out gifts through a raffle or some other means, but that year they wanted to have a contest for the gifts. One of her colleagues in all seriousness suggested a wet T-shirt contest. It was one of the few times Lisa mentioned human resources to ensure that discussion went no further. It wasn't a time when going to HR was likely to yield positive results, and women who reported to HR were often discriminated against further, and some even lost their jobs for pointing out bad behavior.

Usually, Lisa dealt with it by keeping her head down, working six and seven days a week for many years and treating people well regardless of how they treated her. She protected her reputation and worked to add value to each company, regardless of the circumstances. On a good day, she could make a joke about the bad behavior, not to condone but rather to avoid becoming isolated in a world where isolation was deadly to a career. While it's much better today, the problem isn't solved, and discrimination still exists in some pockets. It's frustrating and disappointing, and for most women, it takes a lot of unnecessary energy just to deal with it.

While she faced many challenges through the years, Lisa's overall career has been very successful. She rose to the executive level on Wall Street, and then when she needed a better work-life balance after having children, she left Wall Street for a Fortune 500 information services company called Thomson Reuters, where she led a global white-glove consulting team for some of their most demanding and complex clients. When the kids grew up, she was free to explore again, and with each change she tapped the network that she had carefully built through the years. She moved to a top accounting firm, and then she decided to move into technology. With her standard resolute and focused determination, she sought an exciting company where she can bring all the knowledge and skills she's gained through the years to help the company advance its strategy. Again tapping her network, she eventually found her current company, Cognizant, a top-200 company with a very positive culture that provides digital solutions to advance businesses.

If she could go back and do it all over again, her only wish is that at times she would have been stronger in the face of discrimination, but we can only deal with these situations based on our experience and knowledge at the time. However, Lisa is a strong leader today, and the impact of her leadership will only grow in the coming years, because every time a woman gets into a real, non-token, senior leadership position, cultures shift in a way that is more accepting to women. And every time a woman gets on a corporate board, great and small gender-friendly shifts will occur. So undoubtedly, all of those painful, distracting, and sometimes demeaning experiences will be used for good as Lisa continues her leadership and governance roles in the business world.

Words of Wisdom from Lisa to You

- Focus on the culture of a company that you are thinking of working for, because it makes a huge difference.
- It's okay to change your career path and to change companies to find a better fit, achieve a higher level, or just to feel valued at a different level.
- Being kind to the people you work with is the most important thing you can do. From janitors to the C-Suite, being kind to people as a human being and not forgetting that we are all human is very important. Sometimes the smallest gesture will touch a person in a way that they will not forget. And if you're having a bad day, being kind to someone else is one of the best ways to make your own day better and theirs too.

1. Loosvelt, D. (2020, August 26). *State of Gender Equality on Wall Street in 5 Charts.* Vault. https://www.vault.com/blogs/in-the-black-vaults-finance-careers-blog/state-of-gender-equality-on-wall-street-in-5-charts.

ROBERTA SYDNEY

Independent Board Member and
former CEO
Location: Boston, Massachusetts,
United States

MY HIGHEST ACHIEVEMENTS

1. Founding my own company and being a successful CEO, delivering outstanding returns to my investors in the real estate development industry through multiple challenging market cycles
2. Initiating and launching a new business for State Street Global Advisors into the RIA Market
3. Attaining number-one market share in mortgages for the first time in Baybank's history

STUMBLING BLOCKS OR STEPPING-STONES

Soon after Roberta Sydney joined our network, she stepped up to co-lead our education subcommittee, and she quickly became known for her diligence and commitment to excellence. Arranging a continuing education program for a group of high-achieving, Harvard-educated women is not an easy task, but Roberta assumed the challenge, and soon our programs were extremely organized with timely content. Our speakers were Fortune 500 CEOs and board members, the perfect teachers for our members. There was no fanfare, just matter-of-fact deliverables that Roberta set for herself and the network. That's how Roberta is. She is intuitive about the gaps in leadership around her, and she is willing to give of herself by stepping in and doing the hard work that is required to fill those gaps. She did it for us, and she's been doing it her entire life, as circumstances in her early childhood required more of her than most.

When Roberta was only 13, her mother had a debilitating stroke, leaving her an invalid with five children, ages one and a half to 14. Roberta understood what needed to be done, and she began to pick up many of the responsibilities for the household and her younger siblings. This was not the teenage life she had imagined, but it didn't matter. There was work to be done, and someone had to do it. It was a choice but not one that she spent much time considering, as her father had taught Roberta and her siblings early on the value of hard work and a sense of duty to do things that make the world a better place. Her father not only taught them in words, but he also taught them by example. He had no hobbies or leisurely pastimes. His life was work, the community, and family. With a deeply ingrained sense of responsibility, Roberta was there to catch the baton when it fell after her mother's stroke, but little did she know that was only the first of many decisions she would face in the coming years to help her family.

In college, Roberta studied literature and languages. She loved languages almost as much as she loved taking charge, and she initially thought that she would use this as a foundation for a career in international law. She was fortunate to receive an internship at a law firm early on that afforded her a closer look at the legal profession. She soon realized that the attorneys were typically not the ones with the final decision-making authority, and that settled it. The legal path was not her path.

After earning an MBA from Harvard, Roberta went to work in financial services, where the lessons came hard and fast. She learned that the industry at the time had a serious glass ceiling for women and that her style didn't always fit. She brought her whole heart to the work and with it her natural mode of straightforward conversation, questioning the status quo and politely, respectfully but diligently speaking truth to power. It turns out that power doesn't always want to hear the truth, and Roberta was told that she would need to change to be successful. While she wasn't resistant to communicating differently, she was resistant to changing her personality, and she decided that in order to bring her best talents to the workplace, she had to find a workplace that was better suited for her.

Having made that decision, she left the organization and went back to school for a second graduate degree, this time a master of science from the Massachusetts Institute of Technology (MIT), in real estate development.

She put her degree to use soon thereafter by joining a West Coast, active-adult retirement community developer. In that role Roberta applied her no-nonsense approach to provide deep, hands-on, strategic operational real estate planning and feasibility recommendations supporting go/no-go decisions, and generating business and marketing plans. She also successfully negotiated loans totaling $711 million.

The fit was certainly better, but it didn't last, because the US economy took a deep dive in 1987, and real estate was one of the hardest hit industries. Roberta and her colleagues did their best to keep functioning despite the daily calls from tenants who could no longer pay rent, many of whom had to file for bankruptcy. Roberta recalls going to an industry conference, and it seemed no one was attending the sessions. The times were so difficult that her industry colleagues skipped the formalities and went straight to the bar.

Eventually she left the development company and went back into finance, where she made her way to State Street Global Advisors. This time, her style was valued. She pioneered and launched a new division to market the firm's institutional-grade services to the registered investment adviser market for their high-net-worth clients. In the very first year, she secured over $175MM in new assets, and all was going well when family responsibilities would call her again.

It was her father who needed her. Only in his 60s, he had developed Parkinson's disease, and someone was needed to run the family construction business. Roberta made the choice again to do what needed to be done. She worked nights, weekends, and one day a week in the family business while still maintaining and successfully executing her role at State Street, but the two roles were too much for one person, and Roberta chose what was best for the family. She relinquished her position at State Street and went home to run the family business.

If working in a corporate business can be challenging, working in a family business can be excruciating, as business decisions and emotions are inevitably entangled. The work, direction, and culture can become complicated and painstaking. Still, she was able to manage the business until it was time to close it down, but she had learned something very important about herself. She had learned that smaller companies were nimbler and fit her style better. Furthermore, all the leadership lessons she had learned while working in large public corporations were helpful as she ran and grew smaller businesses.

With that, Roberta chose not to reenter a large, corporate environment but instead decided to found her own real estate development company in 1999. She set a vision and a strategy and worked hard to help her employees learn what an important part they played in achieving the vision of delivering outstanding rental experiences to every commercial and residential tenant in the portfolio. What started as an 18-month experiment turned into 18 years with a successful exit. Today, Roberta is continuing her mantra of doing what is needed as she serves on several corporate boards. In these roles, she can share her insights and relentless pursuit of making things better, and she is also able to share some of her important life lessons, and these she is also willing to share with us.

WORDS OF WISDOM FROM ROBERTA TO YOU

- First, and most important, I hope that you embrace that life is precious, and health is not guaranteed. Try to take neither people nor time for granted. Be willing to do what is necessary. Be a good citizen and make the world better by stepping into the gap when it's needed and doing the work yourself when others cannot or will not.

- Also, I encourage you to leave an organization where you do not fit in. Trust your gut about company culture fit, and if it isn't right, be fearless and make a change. And, when it gets hard, take care of yourself. Do things that put fuel back in your tank. Maintain your self-care routines, from haircuts and exercise to allowing for leisure time. Stay involved with groups and forums where you can talk to others outside of your normal circles and share ideas and draw inspiration.

- Finally, embrace your team. Recognize how important they are in getting through the hard times. You're not alone. You can get through it together.

VALERIE ROBERT

Global Head of Human Resources for
Nespresso
Chair and Global Board Director for
Coaching in Organization,
International Coaching Federation
Location: Geneva, Switzerland

MY HIGHEST ACHIEVEMENTS

1. Balancing successfully my personal and professional lives while bringing up two children (now young adults who are happy, balanced, and successful in their own way) and making a dual career work
2. Making an impact on business by leading broadscale business and cultural transformation globally, leveraging my organization assessment and design mastery into driving the strategic agenda, shaping culture for success, resulting in accelerated levels of performance for the business, the organization, its teams, and employees
3. Making an impact to growth of individuals as I was supporting and coaching leadership teams and business leaders during transition for success

STUMBLING BLOCKS OR STEPPING-STONES

Born in Paris, France, Valerie Robert is a French and Swiss national who has worked in France, the United Kingdom, Pakistan, and the United States, and who is currently working in Geneva, Switzerland. She speaks French and fluent English, but with a beautiful French accent. Valerie has a sense of clarity about relationships, work, and life in general. She has a very natural acceptance of who she is, inside and out, which comes across in every conversation and also translates into a unique authenticity.

Valerie's clarity was already in progress when she graduated from one of Europe's top business schools. As she entered the workforce, she knew that she wanted to get into a company and have the opportunity to be chief human resources officer. She wasn't exactly sure what that path would mean and wasn't even completely sure what the job would entail when she made it, but that's what she wanted. She had a dream, and she pursued it with focus. Today, she is the global head of HR for a major corporation, just as she had envisioned so many years ago.

One thing Valerie understood even before she went into the business world was that the role of HR should be very strategic and grounded in the business. This business sense has helped her lead the HR function throughout her career, and to also get identified as someone who was also able to lead strategy and operations. Early on, one of her bosses at Procter and Gamble asked her about her career plans, and when Valerie told him what she wanted to do, he explained that while she had an MBA, she knew nothing about life, and that if she wanted to be a global head of HR, she needed to manage people. He said that she needed to understand what the plant was all about and learn the manufacturing organization, because as an HR leader she was going to manage people, and the majority of the people she would manage would be in plants around the world. He wanted her to go manage people and learn to be a team operator. And he sent her to run her own team of people in another plant.

This was one of Valerie's hardest work and life experiences. She not only had to get completely out of her comfort zone and learn to run an organization of mostly male manufacturing shift workers who didn't want their wives to know that they were working for a woman, but she also had to do so while living in a separate city from her husband.

With wisdom and hindsight, Valerie now treasures that early defining professional experience. She learned some of her most valuable work and life lessons during this time, and she even grew to love the work. It was exciting and challenging, and if she had not been married, she might still be there today. One of the many lessons Valerie learned during this time was the importance of environment and culture. She learned to help shape the culture and create an environment where employees could thrive. She also learned to use good critical thinking skills, pay attention to shifts in the landscape both personally and professionally, and be willing to adapt. She had to take chances and learn on the fly. There were things that no one can prepare you for, like having an employee show up drunk in the lab, having to figure out the integration of 18,000 employees after an acquisition, or having to manage a family and personal life in two cities.

Balancing her personal and professional life was always a priority for Valerie, who like many successful women worked long hours and still managed a family with young children. With global responsibilities, she often had to work late at night to hold meetings across various time zones. She remembers one night when she was so tired that she told her colleagues that she needed three hours of sleep, and then she could get back on the phone. During this phase she had teenagers who not only needed their parents for normal life circumstances but who both wanted to play professional tennis, which meant that the parents had to organize their lives around their children's tennis practices and competitions in addition to their work schedules. There is a need for strong organization that comes with high-level global jobs, and Valerie and her husband communicated a lot to make it work.

They made some agreements early on that helped them as a couple and as parents. First, they established family rituals, including a twice-per-year time of reflection and discussion about their relationship, their choices, and their lives. They shared what was working and what needed to be adjusted. They made decisions together and then accepted the consequences of their decisions. When the children were young, one of those was that the first parent who had a business trip planned had priority, and the other parent could not travel the same day so they'd be home that evening. They also chose to establish rituals in the family, such as shopping and cooking together on Sunday to prepare all the evening meals for the week, and then to eat together as a family each evening. They enjoyed a time on Friday evenings for the family to sit with a beverage and discuss the week. These rituals put a heartbeat in the family that they treasured and that helped through the long hours and dedication to both work and family.

Unlike many working women, Valerie didn't feel guilty about being a working mom, even when she and her husband had to live and work in different cities, which happened more than once as they navigated two successful careers. Valerie's own mother had no other choice than to work all her life, even with young kids at home, as unexpectedly, when Valerie was only seven, her father passed away in an automotive accident. That life tragedy shaped her in many ways, including an understanding that children can adjust and be healthy and happy with mothers who work, and, even more important, that life is precious and there is no guarantee of tomorrow.

All these experiences have shaped who Valerie is today. She chose early on that no matter what she faced she was going to be herself. She would succeed or fail, but either way she wasn't going to try to pretend to be something that she wasn't. She committed to do her best, and if it wasn't good enough then she would move on and do something else. This took a lot of pressure off and allowed her to stay focused on the issues in front of her rather than on what others thought of her. When you talk to Valerie you quickly experience this approach, as it is immediately clear that she is comfortable with who she is and that you are experiencing her natural, comfortable, and authentic self. She's the kind of person that you would want to sit down with and get some life advice, which is exactly what she agreed to share with all who read this book.

WORDS OF WISDOM FROM VALERIE TO YOU

- I encourage you to take educated risks both at home and at work. Go ahead and make choices, and be willing to accept the consequences.
- Figure out which things are in your control and which things are not, and let go of the things that are not in your control.
- Be curious and courageous. Think things through, form an opinion, and then be willing to share it.
- Try to get into an environment where you are not judged.
- Surround yourself with mentors and friends who can help you along the way, but regardless of what you face, choose to be yourself.
- Accept that life—and you—are not perfect.
- Find the right partner for you. That one choice can make all the difference.
- Finally, remember that in the end, your tombstone will not say anything about your career. Stay focused on the things that matter.

PATRICIA (TRISH) HURTER, PhD

Pharmaceutical Executive, Chemical
Engineer, Drug
Discovery and Development
Location: Cambridge, Massachusetts,
United States

MY HIGHEST ACHIEVEMENTS

1. Helping to grow Vertex to a $40 billion-plus company while bringing five breakthrough therapies to the market
2. Becoming CEO of Lyndra and accelerating progress of product design, manufacturing, and clinical trials to enable a potential launch, in 2023, of the first product
3. Coaching and mentoring many individuals who have done well in their careers and who have also become a fantastic network of wonderful people who can be mutually supportive

STUMBLING BLOCKS OR STEPPING-STONES

Skara Glen's Machu Picchu (Machu Picchu) is the name of one of the horses co-owned by Trish Hurter. He is an Olympic-level jumping horse who recently won Horse of the Year in Ireland. Horses like Machu Picchu are bred to perform at the highest possible level, and if they aren't resting, performing, or preparing to perform, they are likely to become unfulfilled, unhappy, or unruly. When it comes to leaders, we often see the same.

Using horses as an analogy for talent, there are backyard pleasure horses and sport horses bred to perform as elite athletes. The backyard pleasure horses are the corporate B-players: "These capable, steady performers are the best supporting actors of the business world."[1] They are the majority in the middle. Then there are the elite athletes bred to perform at the top levels of the sport. These are the A-players, the "stars" and "top 10%"[2] of corporate talent. A-players, like thoroughbreds, need to be running, jumping, or resting. They need to perform, to push themselves, to give it everything they have inside of them, and this is where Trish and Machu Picchu are the same. It is in their DNA to perform at the highest levels.

From a long line of South Africans, Trish grew up in Durban, South Africa. She went to university there and received an undergraduate degree in chemical engineering from the University of KwaZulu-Natal in Durban. She thought she would start out with a job in a factory after graduation, but then she decided to get her master's degree. That is when she had the opportunity to go to the United States. Another South African postdoctoral student was recruiting for West Virginia University, and he lured Trish with full tuition for her master's degree. She thought that sounded like a great deal and was soon on a plane headed for the US. She imagined what the US would be like, but when she landed in Morgantown, West Virginia, she was taken aback by her surroundings. She expected it to be much more modern than South Africa, but in many ways, it was relatively backward. Nonetheless, she settled in and spent the next 15 months working on a master's degree in mechanical engineering. Before she finished, she decided to keep going and pursue a PhD, and being the high performer that she is, she wanted to find the best place in the country for a doctorate in chemical engineering, which she decided was at MIT, in Boston.

After receiving her doctorate, Trish started her career as a scientist, but it didn't take long for her stellar performance and hard work to set her apart from others. She quickly moved into leadership and then made a series of moves to bigger organizations, each time gaining in responsibility and stature. When she was hired at Vertex Pharmaceuticals, she felt that she was in a great place and ended up spending nearly 15 years there. She made her way to Senior Vice President, Pharmaceutical & Preclinical Sciences, and helped the organization grow to $40 billion in revenue by bringing multiple drugs through the regulatory process, leading teams in clinical research and development, and conceiving and executing the world's first FDA-approved continuous manufacturing facility, among other things. It was good. Trish was working on interesting things with people she liked and respected. After a time, Trish reached a point where she was unable to advance any further. She had been successful both as a scientist and a leader, but for whatever reason, she didn't see herself getting onto the most senior executive team. A-players need a clear track to run on, and Trish had come upon a gate that she could not open.

Eventually, she made the very difficult decision to retire. She still loved the company and still had many lifelong friends, but she wanted to learn and grow in new ways and to make room for those coming up behind her. To ensure there was a smooth transition, Trish gave a one-year notice of her retirement. For the first six months, very few people knew she planned to retire, so it was business as usual, but the last six months were different. Vertex officially announced Trish was leaving and transitioned her responsibilities to the people who were taking over. At that point, she didn't have a whole lot to do, and this was uncomfortable for her. It made her feel irrelevant, and she found herself slipping into depression.

That's when the head of HR came to Trish and told her that the company had hired a vendor to run a business simulation for leadership training, and they wanted her to attend. Trish couldn't understand why they would pay for her to go since she was retiring, but they thought she could add perspective to those getting trained, and since Trish didn't have a lot to do, she agreed.

It was a three-day business simulation, and they were working in teams. Even though it was just a simulation, Trish had so much fun at this. She was working with a bunch of smart people; they were competing, and they were working in teams. She found herself energized, excited, and wanting to win the competition. That is when the lightbulb went on. Trish realized that she loves working with other people and working in a team, and she just might not be the kind of person who could sit around without something exciting and engaging going on. She thought about the simulation and compared it with her retirement plan to devote time to yoga, taking courses in languages, and joining a couple of boards, and upon careful review, she knew retirement might not work out.

Soon after this experience, Trish met the CEO of Lyndra Therapeutics, she thought to discuss a potential board role, but to her surprise, she was presented with an opportunity to become the CEO of Lyndra. The more she researched, the more she knew it was a really great fit for her background. Lyndra is a company spun out of the Langer labs at MIT. They have developed an innovative new dosage-delivery mechanism that allows people to take medicine orally once a week or once a month instead of every day. It is transformational in terms of how people take medicine. Imagine someone with Alzheimer's having to remember to take multiple medications every day. With Lyndra's dosage method, a caregiver can stop by once a week or once a month and take care of the medication delivery. Some of the specific programs they are working on include malaria eradication in Africa, and a monthly oral contraceptive for women. It's a great company with interesting and unique products that will change how people take medicine and help them to stay healthy. Instead of thinking about curing a disease, Lyndra is focused on keeping people healthy in the first place.

Looking back, Trish's only regret is that she didn't make the leap from Vertex sooner, but if she had she may have missed such a perfect fit with Lyndra. It is all working out. She gets to do exciting work with a great team, and even though she didn't retire, she still manages to have time to serve on Synlogic Inc.'s corporate board and, of course, she still makes time for her horses.

Trish has always had something very compelling to do besides work. In South Africa, it was sailing. She sailed dinghies and ocean-racing yachts, but ever since she was a little girl, she always wanted to ride horses. She always thought that when she grew up, she was going to have a horse, so when she received her very first promotion in her very first company, as soon as her raise came through, she bought her first horse and started taking lessons. The next thing she knew, her horse count grew, and her farm count grew, and now she has two farms and six horses. She rides every morning before work, even though it means she is up and out the door before 5:00 a.m., and she rides all weekend. With just a quick search of the internet, you will see Trish on one of her horses, jumping, or the world class show-jumping rider she supports winning Nations Cups and international competitions around the world. The scene may change from the corporate arena to the horse arena, but the key ingredients that keep Trish excited and engaged are the same: a great team, a challenging competition, and a chance to win.

WORDS OF WISDOM FROM TRISH TO YOU

Just do it! If you feel like you might need to make a change, you're probably way overdue for making a change. Don't be afraid to take the plunge and do something different.

---

1. DeLong, Thomas J., and Vineeta Vijayaraghavan. "Let's Hear It for B Players." *Harvard Business Review* 81, no. 6 (June 2003), 3.
2. Ibid., 4.

LAURA KIERNAN

CEO, High Touch Investor Relations
Location: New York, New York, United States

MY HIGHEST ACHIEVEMENTS

1. Founding and building High Touch Investor Relations while supporting founders as an adviser and Angel Investor.
2. Helping public companies triple in valuation (UI, WWE, HWDC, and VQSLF) using my five-step Transformative IR Plan.
3. Guest lecturing at Northeastern University, Fordham Gabelli School of Management, and GIBS Business School South Africa, to undergraduate and graduate students.

STUMBLING BLOCKS OR STEPPING-STONES

Listening to Laura Kiernan's podcast, *Raising Billions*, is like going to graduate school for investor relations, especially concerning raising capital and activist investor tactics, and understanding finance and management. Her subject matter expertise is deep and impressive, which matches people's experience of Laura herself. She has an authentic, pleasant, but serious style that exudes both quality and mastery of her industry. Her expertise has established her in one of the most competitive financial environments in the world, and it has taken her into some very high-level roles at companies, like Ubiquiti, World Wrestling Entertainment (WWE), Playtex Products, Harry Winston, Revlon, and more, often guiding companies to double and triple their valuation. She has also been recognized by her industry colleagues, being named #2 Best Investor Relations in Technology, Media and Telecom Mid-Small Cap, as voted by the global buy-side and sell-side in 2019, and #3 Best Investor Relations in Technology, Media and Telecom Mid-Small Cap, as voted by the global buy-side in 2020, according to *Institutional Investor*.

Her ability to establish herself and overcome difficulties started early. Laura grew up in Colorado, but for as long as she can remember, she aspired to work in Manhattan. However, getting there required a big initial choice to break out of a parochial family dynamic. Her parents were old fashioned. She had four brothers and three sisters and the mindset was that the boys were going to go to college and the girls were going to become wives and mothers. Therefore, any money that could go toward college would be allocated to the boys. Since the girls were going to be wives and mothers, they didn't need an education. It just wasn't a good use of money. If she wanted to go to college, she would have to pay for it herself. And that is exactly what she did. She was determined to work in the big city and to prove to the family that she was just as smart and capable as the boys, especially her twin brother.

Choosing to go to college and paying for it on her own was extremely difficult for a young adult. This early challenge was one of the biggest in her life so far, as she had to work 30 hours a week, borrow money, and apply for grants and scholarships just to make it. This was all in addition to completing her university coursework.

Fortunately, it paid off, as she landed an amazing job at Philip Morris International right out of college, allowing her to pay off all her debt within two years. This first job in finance with a large international consumer goods company enabled Laura to establish herself at a young age, all while earning her CPA license. During this time, she also traveled extensively throughout the US, Europe, and Asia.

Today, Laura has a husband of over 25 years and two teenage children to help her through difficult times, but in her youth, she relied on her faith for support. Her parents were not very religious, but Laura had an interest in religion from the age of five. She would either go to church with a neighbor or go by herself, but one way or another, she was going to get there. Through the years and even today, her faith has kept her grounded and humble and always wanting to know and see the best in others.

After establishing herself in the business world, Laura faced other challenges. One was managing up. With a youthful appearance, long blond hair, and Colorado background, business leaders wondered why she was the one telling them how to run their business from the financial market standpoint. Tenacious as ever, Laura didn't let this attitude set her back. Just like she found a way to get a college degree, she figured out various ways to help these business leaders in a way they could receive it. Sometimes that meant Laura needed to bring in a seasoned, salt-and-pepper-haired adviser to deliver the message that she was perfectly capable of delivering herself. Other times, she dropped enough breadcrumbs for the leader to pick up the direction and then waited for the leader to share his or her brilliant idea, which Laura reinforced as excellent thinking. Laura is about results, not recognition, and she didn't let the small things get in the way of the big things. She wanted to get the job done and to stay true to her values in the process.

The latter didn't always prove easy. Early on, it meant leaving a good job, because she didn't want to continue to work for a company that sold tobacco, and it also caused her to get fired from one job and to quit another. Laura's measure of success was not and still isn't just having a good job that pays well. Her measures include doing good things for good people, working for companies that do good things, and staying true to herself throughout.

She also learned a lot about leadership on her journey. She learned from the CEO of Playtex to give others important work that requires them to learn new and complex skills. He would leave town and become unavailable before an important investor day or meeting and require the senior team to prepare thoroughly. At first it was terrifying, but then she saw that it was brilliant: as they learned to work together, they had more ownership, and they grew their skills together.

She also learned from working with multiple billionaires that they did not get there by accident. They are rich in perseverance. She has studied and worked with many who persevered, like Vince McMahon of WWE, who filed bankruptcy twice before becoming a billionaire.

Today, Laura has a boutique investor relations firm that focuses on a limited number of public and private company clients. She likes to find unique ways to share the stories of misunderstood and unknown companies and help them find a way to be recognized in the capital markets with fair valuation.

WORDS OF WISDOM FROM LAURA TO YOU

- When it's really hard, like it was for me when I was putting myself through college, just remember to take it one day at a time! It may take a while, but eventually you will get through the difficult times. Also, set boundaries on your values and your time. Others will take as much as you will let them, so you have to know what you need and what you feel good about up front so that you can set and keep your boundaries. Find your internal compass and stay with it.

- Above all, never give up. Never lose hope. You are the driver of your own dream, and if you set your mind to it, you can do it.

GISELLA BENAVENTE

CEO and Managing Partner, KREAB
Perú
Location: Lima, Perú

MY HIGHEST ACHIEVEMENTS

1. Being part of the team that built up four infrastructure-concession companies in a strongly regulated and very complex environment
2. Managing social conflicts involving people protesting with violence on the street
3. Taking over the leadership of commercial, compliance, and corporate communications areas of infrastructure companies with a lawyer background

STUMBLING BLOCKS OR STEPPING-STONES

Gisella (Gigi) Benavente lives in Lima, Perú. It is the political, cultural, financial, and commercial center of the country and the third largest city in the Americas, with a population of almost 9 million.[1] She grew up in Lima, Perú, where her father was in the Navy. He was an officer and joined when he was 16 years old. He traveled around the world and was a leader of many missions.

Her mother was a member of the World Association of Girl Guides and Girl Scouts, the largest volunteer movement in the world dedicated to girls and young women. She joined when she was 10 years old, and Gigi grew up as a member too. Guiding is a way that girls and young women can challenge themselves, put their ideas into action, take part in an amazing range of activities, and gain the skills to confidently navigate their world. They both did what they loved and felt very passionate about. Gigi decided she wanted to be an attorney because she is very passionate about justice. So she went to the University of Lima and obtained both a law degree and a postgraduate degree in corporate communication.

Gigi started her career working as an attorney for BellSouth, but life has a funny way of altering our plans, and it didn't take long for her natural business mindset and budding leadership skills to bring opportunities well beyond legal. Working with and for numerous companies, within the first 10 years of her career, Gigi gained enormous experience in almost all segments of business. She built a commercial area for a multinational company from the ground up, and then she did the same for compliance and corporate communications. She had become the chief compliance officer for a large natural gas distributor and for a highway concession company. She worked in and led teams in legal, community relations, sales, marketing, oversight for back-office functions, and customer service relations. She learned how to build relationships with opinion leaders and government authorities and to represent the company in the press. It was quite a ride, and although she was having clear career successes, she felt she was living in a man's world, and one that was often very difficult.

Women were often treated differently. Sometimes they were ignored, talked over, pushed down, pushed out, and avoided, and other times they were outright harassed, personally and sexually, and it wasn't a time when going to HR would have changed much. Gigi begrudged being treated different from the men when she experienced the personal slights and transgressions, but when she saw it happening to other women, it made her furious.

She has a big heart, and Gigi has always cared deeply about helping others, whether it's volunteering for organizations like Kantaya, an organization that educates and empowers vulnerable children, the Ronald McDonald House, the World Association of Girl Guides and Girl Scouts, or through mentoring younger professionals. So when she found herself with a young mentee who told her of experiences that had her questioning if she could be a mother, Gigi listened carefully.

One example was listening to a young female attorney who had recently been in a meeting with mostly men. She was the expert on the topic at hand, so she started talking to one of the men about the issues. He answered back, but when he did, he was looking at her boss, because he was a man. So, he talked to her boss, and then her boss turned and relayed what he had said as if she weren't there when he said it. She answered the question, and he responded again, not to her but to her boss. This went on during the entire meeting. The mentee went on to share that she didn't think being a great professional and having a family were a good match and that she would have to decide, and she didn't know what she would choose. Gigi asked why she thought this way. She responded that when she observed the female attorneys, they were so behind the men, because they are trying to be all there for work and all there for their children at the same time. They either miss out on the time with their family or they miss out on the best opportunities at work, so eventually it's better to choose.

It made Gigi sad to hear it, and she encouraged her that it was possible, and she also lived it by not allowing work to stop her from living a full life. She married and had three daughters, but, to be fair, it was difficult but possible, if you are careful enough to choose a life partner who shares and respects your career vision. There were times when she was speaking on behalf of her company and had to be in the streets during volatile protests, with men saying all kinds of inappropriate things. It was dangerous and exhausting, but she needed to work, so she kept showing up and doing her job. She remembers a random act of kindness, when during one of these protests, a woman who had been watching brought a chair out to the street for her because Gigi was eight months pregnant.

Her children didn't pause when she needed to focus on work, and her work didn't pause when her children were sick or needed her to attend something. She was offered her first C-Suite position while on maternity leave and considering whether to even return. It was a huge promotion, but she wanted to spend more time with her girls, and a bigger job wouldn't give her more time. She took the promotion and gave all that she had in her to both family and work. As her career progressed, she eventually left the natural gas company and went on to provide strategic consulting to several large corporations. Later, she went internal again, working for an infrastructure organization where she served as head of corporate communications and chief compliance officer, reporting to the CEO, and began working with the board of directors.

Along the way, there were times when the frustration was overwhelming. In one meeting with a colleague, she was so frustrated she started to cry. Her colleague was completely shaken by the emotion and asked what she was doing. Gigi said, "I'm crying because I'm frustrated and sad." He didn't know what to do. He asked why she was doing that, because he didn't think Gigi Benavente cried. She realized then that the image she and other women were having to project wasn't always an accurate image. Women were in a way covering up who they really were to fit into this man's world. It wasn't uncommon for her to be the only woman in a room of 20 business leaders, all men. She would be listening and engaging in the meeting and at the same time analyzing what she needed to do and say to gain the respect and have a voice. There were times in these meetings when one man would look at another and tell him to explain it to Gigi as if she couldn't understand.

Today it's different, but at the time, women who brought up issues of discrimination were told they were just being emotional. So Gigi grew a thick skin, expanded her patience, and strategically found ways to deal with every issue. Then she came to a point when she decided she didn't want to deal with it any longer. She didn't want to step back. She wanted to step forward and do something more meaningful. She just knew in her heart: it didn't have to be like that. So she quit her job and gave herself a year to really think about what she wanted to do with her life. She knew that she wanted quality over quantity, and she also wanted to fulfill some of her lifelong dreams, such as going to Harvard, which she did. When she arrived, she wrote home to her three daughters to let them know that it is never too late to achieve your dreams, because she had dreamed of going there since she was their age.

Gigi figured out what she wanted to do, and today she is the CEO of KREAB Perú, a strategy, communication, and public affairs consultancy founded in Stockholm, in 1970, with a presence in 25 countries and a multidisciplinary team of 500 consultants. She serves on nonprofit boards and also writes columns for two of Perú's most important business media companies, with a goal of influencing business and government leaders to build a better world based on cooperation and common good, and in which we honor the dignity of every human being. She wants to impact her community, and she also wants to demonstrate to her daughters that they are a part of a bigger world where they have a responsibility to contribute and build a better society. She wants them to know that while they must take care of themselves, it should always be with an awareness that they are part of a society and that what they do with their life matters. As it is said, they must know they can be the change they want to see in the world.

WORDS OF WISDOM FROM GISELLA TO YOU

- If you are thinking of growing professionally, your partner must share the same vision. You need someone who truly believes you have the same chances and share home responsibilities equally. It's very, very important who you choose to be your partner in life. If you are not equal at home, it's harder to be able to develop your career, and that's what you show your children.

- You can spend your life searching instead of achieving. The truth is you aren't successful until you decide you are.
- We are a part of an interdependent world in which we need each other. We cannot succeed at the cost of the society we all belong to.
- I believe in energy and that the power is within you. There is no limit on what you are capable of creating for yourself based on your thoughts and responses to life.

---

1. Lima. (2020, December 18). Retrieved December 28, 2020, from https://en.wikipedia.org/wiki/Lima

Chapter 4

Sensemaking

"If you are going through hell, keep going."

—Anonymous

THE FOLLOWING STORIES HAVE AN underlying theme of *sensemaking*, the ongoing process of giving meaning to one's experiences and making sense of ambiguous situations. As a leadership competency, it requires leaders who will intentionally slow down, think strategically, and take a long look at what is happening around them.

Sensemaking involves learning to pick up weak signals, taking time to understand what is happening, and predicting what may be coming around the corner. The work of making sense of circumstances requires leaders who will analyze the work that is being conducted, the people doing the work, the culture, the customers, and the competition in light of the overall vision and strategy and then to ask themselves and their teams, "What does this mean?"

In the 2019 Trends in Executive Development Benchmark Report, Dr. David Peterson,[1] stated it this way:

"...diverse, challenging experiences are perhaps the most critical element of development, but without someone who can help you make sense of it and figure out what you personally need to do with it—coaching, mentoring, peers—the experiences aren't worth much. I think sensemaking, reflection—really deep reflection—are going to be essential for leaders dealing with complexity and change. How do you slow down enough to see the patterns, read signals, and anticipate shifts? Right now, the best way to do that is in community and conversation with others."[2]

In the stories ahead, you will read the experiences of leaders who were blindsided or impacted by internal or external politics, as well as those who called on champions, mentors, coaches, and therapists as valuable resources to help them make sense of what was going on around them and sorting out their own thoughts and emotions.

1. David B. Peterson, PhD, is the current chief catalyst and transformation officer at 7 Paths Forward and the former director of executive coaching and leadership at Google, Inc.
2. Hagemann, B., et. al. (2019). Trends and Their Implications. In *2019 Trends in Executive Development: A Benchmark Report* (p. 17–23). United States: EDA, Inc. & BTS USA, Inc.

Cynthia (Cinny) Murray

CEO, Stanmore Partners
President, Board Member, Advisor to
global retail brands
Location: Naples, Florida, United States

My Highest Achievements

1. President of Chicos, President of FULLBEAUTY Brands; both billion-dollar retail companies
2. Led transformation turnaround at $2 billion retail company Talbots, increasing the stock from $11 to $50, split and settled at $38 in five years
3. Developed and mentored multiple teams and leaders who were promoted and advanced in their careers far beyond their dreams

Stumbling Blocks or Stepping-Stones

Cinny Murray is the type of person that you notice right away in a room full of people. She stands out, but not because she is trying to draw attention to herself. She just has a charisma and presence that draws your attention. If you have a conversation with her, she will focus on learning about you instead of sharing about herself unless you ask, and she doesn't feel the need to speak up during a meeting unless she is leading or you happen to cross one of her passion points. And if you do, she will quickly, knowledgeably, and intelligently weigh in and then step back out of the limelight. It just isn't her style to demand attention, but that doesn't mean she doesn't have it. She remembers people and conversations and reaches out, seemingly out of the blue, to check and see if you are doing okay and whether she can do anything to help you on your journey. It's no wonder that Cinny climbed the corporate ladder in the retail industry quickly, because her heart is big and fearless and her work ethic admirable.

The only thing surprising is that Cinny is in retail at all. What she wanted to study was interior design, but Cinny's father steered her in a different direction. She was an independent and competitive youth, and her father instinctively knew to nourish and channel her natural personality characteristics. If Cinny set her eyes on a target, he was right beside her telling her she could do it over and over. In fact, he said it so many times that Cinny believes most of her success today originated with her parents and the way they guided and encouraged her early on. This, combined with her many years at camp, is where she learned how to live and play on a team. Her mother was a nurse and taught her that everyone in the family needed to be a contributor. Her father was a business executive, so despite her artistic nature, Cinny always valued financial prowess and strategy. The core of their teaching was for Cinny to set a course where she could make a difference in the world.

Growing up in Florida, Cinny attended Pine Crest High School and then moved on to attend Florida State University. Cinny chose the business school with a focus in marketing, as she gravitated to the mix of creative with business fundamentals. There were not many women in the business school, but she didn't care. She enjoyed working with the guys, made many lasting friendships, and today serves on the board of that same business school, where she was inducted into the Florida State Hall of Fame.

After graduation, Cinny and her friend moved to Atlanta to get jobs. Her father was expecting her to get a job at one of the big brands of the time such as IBM or Xerox, but Cinny soon called to share her excitement of her newfound career calling in fashion retail. Dad responded with complete silence, but Cinny was not deterred. She had found the perfect career path. She spent the day helping women gain confidence. Every day was different, which made it exciting. She began in smaller specialty stores, which allowed Cinny to learn every part of running a single retail operation—displays, windows, purchasing, inventory control, customer service, and every other part of running a business—and she made quick work of the management track. Cinny credits this early experience of being so hands-on as a key piece to her understanding the fundamentals to success early in her career.

Cinny caught the eye of a woman who was a senior executive in the industry, and she helped Cinny learn the ropes. No one asked her to mentor Cinny, but she saw her talent and her heart and decided that with a little help, Cinny could go a long way. And she was right. Cinny worked her way up through multiple name-brand retail chains. Cinny gravitated toward companies in distress that needed rebuilding, and built her reputation on successfully rebuilding retail businesses.

She was hired as president of Chico's because of her reputation of successful turnaround results. She began that turnaround by requiring her leaders to spend time on the store sales floor to learn from the customers, lessons she learned from early days of being on the sales floor. She is a huge believer in always starting with the customer you are hired to serve.

Chico's was an organization worth $1 billion, and Cinny was primarily responsible for turning around the company's biggest brand, which had fallen off track. She was outwardly brave yet inwardly processing the responsibility of making a decision that would move many zeros in the wrong direction. As a public company, this pressure never left. Her decisions impacted the company's stock directly. She was always transparent with her senior team. She would go to the board to discuss direction and strategy and then come back to the senior teams and say, "Okay, this is what we have to do; lets figure it out," and then they worked together to get the job done. Cinny's authentic love for the customer and her ability to hire, develop, and empower her leaders provided a culture where they were able to deliver an immediate turnaround to the business.

Another thing that Cinny credits for her connection with people was her mother's insistence that she start volunteering early in her adult life. She told Cinny that she had a nice life but many people have had a more challenging journeys in life. So at 20 years old, she helped Cinny get involved in volunteering, and that is why to this day she's a huge champion for women of domestic abuse and alcoholism. Now when she's in front of a team or a crowd, she sees them through a broader lens. She knows the statistics for women who are impacted by abuse, and she keeps that in mind by offering compassion when people are struggling.

Though her compassion never leaves, she still had to lead the businesses in a profitable way, which often meant that she had to make difficult decisions and reduce expenses. She did that with as much gentleness and care as she could, but she still made the hard decisions quickly and strategically to ensure the company's financial success and long-term sustainability. She learned she had to hone her leadership skills and at times soften or change her approach.

One of the more difficult experiences Cinny went through was learning that not everyone in the companies she worked for was committed to her success. Having participated in teams in her younger years at camp, she couldn't understand why everyone on the same team would not be supportive of a teammate. It just didn't make sense to her. So she hired a world-class coach who had worked with some extremely high-profile leaders, and started the hard work of learning about herself and helping her team. She had him conduct interviews to figure out what Cinny might be doing to cause others not to be supportive and to help her figure out who was really on the team and who was not on board.

She learned that some people were not comfortable with her direct approach, but the biggest insight was that while she was busy trying to fix the business, her focus made peers feel left out of her decision process. By digging in and being open, she was able to learn and then to sit down and have real and open conversations with each person to get feedback. She and the team had to be willing to communicate a lot and to be open and transparent. It was uncomfortable, and it took a while. The importance of self-awareness was a key lesson for Cinny.

Her team learned of their own blind spots and how to improve as leaders, with Cinny leading the way, openly speaking about areas that she would be focusing on to improve her leadership. They had to learn executive courage, and to own areas that needed improvement in them rather than pass by the issue on as part of the corporate fabric. They had to change and reinvent themselves as leaders. There was a lot of discomfort, but they became a better team and better leaders, and developing leaders became a passion for Cinny. She saw its power to transform and after that experience only hired leaders willing to grow as individuals and business leaders.

One of the things Cinny learned about herself was that she had to show her more vulnerable side. She had an "I've got this" persona that wasn't showing the whole picture and held others at arm's length. She had a huge heart but came up the ranks at a time when leaders were taught never to let anyone see you cry. It was a lesson learned late, but it was life changing. It was more fun to lead from the heart versus from a corporate agenda.

She also had to learn to accept a compliment rather than deflect it. Her coach once helped her understand the impact of her deflection after a young employee approached her after an all-company address and complimented her speech. She immediately pushed back, letting him know that it was a team effort, but her coach encouraged her to respond differently. He told Cinny that it took a lot of courage for that young man to come all the way to the front of the auditorium to give her a compliment and that she didn't receive it. She understood and made the adjustment.

Today, Cinny leads her own company as an adviser to retail businesses. She also continues to volunteer, serve on corporate boards, and take care of her family and friends. Ironically, it turns out she was able to have a career in interior design after all. It's all in how you look at it: her interior design just happens to be in the form of companies and people instead of houses and rooms.

Words of Wisdom from Cinny to You

Don't expect when you're in a leadership position to have all the answers; just know how to resource people and surround yourself with a team and mentor that will be honest and real with you. There is a lot of pressure at the top, and it is hard to have awareness of how you are showing up to others. We all need an advocate and a partner to listen when you need it and to guide you through issues and provide feedback so you can improve as a leader.

ROSIE BICHARD

Senior Equity Analyst, Lofoten Asset Management
Location: London, England, United Kingdom

MY HIGHEST ACHIEVEMENTS

1. Becoming one of the top alpha generators at my previous firm for more than a decade and a trusted partner to the rest of the investment team, delivering for clients over the long term
2. Gaining the respect and confidence of many members of senior management of our investee companies, enabling me to have in-depth, strategic conversations about the future of their business
3. Mentoring and advising many younger colleagues and others over the years, many of whom have gone on to have extremely successful and fulfilling careers

STUMBLING BLOCKS OR STEPPING-STONES

Committed, thoughtful in approach, and results-oriented, Rosie Bichard rises to the top quickly in whatever endeavor she pursues. She's serious but with a warm and focused manner. Together, these traits explain why she has had an exciting career in investment management, calling the shots on consumer sector holdings and hosting strategy discussions with senior management of investee companies.

Today Rosie is the senior equity analyst at Lofoten, a privately owned fund-management business with $2 billion of client assets. She is also co-president of WomenExecs on Boards and is on the Independent Governance Committee for Royal London, a UK life and pensions company with US$190 billion. This is part of the UK Financial Conduct Authority's (FCA), oversight framework for the pensions industry, with a particular focus on providing value for money for scheme members. She was educated at Cambridge University, worked extensively in Latin America, and speaks fluent French, Spanish, and Italian. She might sound a little superhuman, but Rosie still has to stop her Zoom calls to go get her son from the bus just like all the other working parents. Being a parent is one of the reasons Rosie left a successful position in a much larger firm to join Lofoten. Fortunately, she has found that she enjoys the smaller firm, not only for its flexibility but also for the work that allows her to go far beyond analyzing potential investments to develop a broader remit.

Rosie didn't always intend to go into finance. Her university education was in modern languages, but a summer internship at Arthur Anderson gave her some direction, and she set her sights on Latin American investment banking. Progressing quickly, Rosie worked for several firms and soon moved into investment management, which she found better suited her skill set and long-term viewpoint. Over time, she developed her expertise from Latin America to cover global equities and Environmental, Social, and Corporate Governance (ESG).

Navigating the financial markets is both exciting and daunting. Rosie gained a good reputation as an analyst and soon had a great job choosing the best consumer stocks around the world on a three-to-five-year view. She spent her time analyzing companies, learning their competitive advantages, and assessing their leadership and strategy. She became quite good at choosing the best companies to invest in and was a trusted partner to many of their most senior leaders. As she excelled, her performance at her organization was recognized, and all could see that her career was on a great path. Still, Rosie did not take her success for granted. She remained focused and was diligent to stay on top of every company she recommended. Unfortunately, investors, board members, and lenders alike can sometimes get blindsided due to poor or flat-out dishonest leadership, and that is what happened to Rosie.

One of the stocks Rosie had recommended was a company that was new to the market. She believed in their story, which was all about women around the world buying affordable jewelry for themselves. At first, her recommendation looked golden, as shortly after its Initial Public Offering (IPO), the stock performed quite strongly. But soon there was a crisis of confidence in the fundamentals of the company as commodity prices were rising quickly. The shares became volatile and began a downward track.

Rose was not comfortable. She suspected something was wrong, and since her firm was a large shareholder, she arranged for several meetings with management to share concerns and pursue answers. Only a few quarters after its IPO, the jewelry company announced the sudden resignation of the CEO and revealed that its financial guidance was not accurate; sales hadn't been as reported, and profits were going to be cut significantly. Rosie was on holiday with her family when the news came out and the shares collapsed. She felt horrible, but she had had no idea about the numbers being inflated. Still, there was a big loss for her firm's clients on this stock, which affected all of the funds' performance. She kicked herself for months afterwards.

In the financial world, compensation is the currency of success. Once a year, it's all down in black and white. Fortunately, the majority of her recommendations had done well that year, particularly the larger ones, and her longer-term performance was still strong, so she was apprehensive but hopeful when she went to her boss for her annual compensation review. However, that year, they focused only on that one loss, and the news was bad. Rosie was stunned, and she left the office confused and upset.

She took a few days to gather her thoughts and her arguments, and went back for a second discussion. Her boss read the reviewers' comments, and they were all about the loss. It was harsh and painful, and no one stood up for her, as the whole firm was going through a tough year. Rosie thought long and hard about whether or not to remain with a company that had such a narrow focus on success, but her internal competitiveness wouldn't let her leave it at that. She decided to prove herself again. With increased focus, Rosie took her performance to a new level, and when she did finally leave the company six years later, she was the top-ranked analyst.

This painful career experience wasn't about the money. It was the lack of appreciation and perceived value for all of the good things that she was contributing. But the hard times, the failures, and the setbacks are where we typically learn the most, and it ultimately made Rosie an even better analyst. It also taught her that when the chips are down, she had to look out for herself, because the courage of her peers might fail. In the years following the incident, several colleagues told her that they thought the firm had been unfair, but it was too late. When their voices needed to be heard, they were silent.

The whole experience made Rosie better in the long run. So when the opportunity came, and she was on the other side of the table, she did not stay silent. One of her female colleagues had a peer who pushed her out of her job, and she asked Rosie to go with her to a hearing after she left. Rosie could see—everyone could see—that the other fund manager was trying to take the large fund away from her colleague, but she also knew that it would have been safer to keep quiet. However, the right thing to do was to give evidence about her colleague's good character try to help her achieve a better outcome. And that's what she did.

After her big setback, Rosie needed friends who felt loyal and authentic. She found a group of colleagues from various departments and levels across the company who were runners like her and began to join them for a Thursday, noontime run. This routine and these colleagues were a major help through the years that followed. They felt like her team as they supported each other through trials and triumphs, and when she left, it was this team that she was saddest to leave.

For most successful leaders, there are pivotal moments that change us. The harder they are, the more strength they have to either break us or make us better. Ultimately, which way we go depends on our own determination and mindset. Rosie's desire to prove herself and show the company her value made her better, instead of bitter. And some lessons just keep on giving, as today she passes on her experience to those she mentors and uses it both in her executive role and in her board positions.

WORDS OF WISDOM FROM ROSIE TO YOU

- Go with your passion. Although it's important to try to do things outside your comfort zone and to keep learning, you will be at your best when you're doing something that you really care about and that you're good at.
- While we can all do more, the main focus of your life needs to be what really speaks to you and what you care about. You'll know when you find it.

DORLISA FLUR

Corporate Director and Strategic
Adviser
Location: Charlotte, North Carolina,
United States

MY HIGHEST ACHIEVEMENTS

1. Graduating first in class at Duke, in accelerated 3-2 program (BS and MBA)
2. Making partner at McKinsey & Company, Inc., first woman elected in Southeast (over 20 years); best moment when client CEO arranged surprise celebration
3. Being promoted to chief merchant at Family Dollar Stores, Inc., first official C-title role with $3 billion-plus gross margin P&L budget

STUMBLING BLOCKS OR STEPPING-STONES

Dorlisa left Duke University with an MBA and a ranking of number one in her class. She was a hardworking problem solver and a perfect recruit for a global management consulting firm that is well known for helping leading organizations tackle complex problems and drive transformational change on major strategy and performance-improvement issues. She ultimately spent nearly 16 years in the organization working with clients from multiple industries and that touched almost every part of their businesses. Eventually she decided that she wanted to transition into industry and take on direct operating roles, rather than watching and advising from the sidelines.

She left the firm to join Family Dollar Stores, Inc., where she held five senior operating roles over her eight-year tenure, ultimately ending up as vice chair, strategy and chief administrative officer. She enjoyed working for this high-growth, Fortune 500 public company, and was especially proud of when she was promoted to chief merchandising officer. This role in retail is similar to chief operating officer in other industries, as it oversees the heart of the retailer's buying and selling operations. She had responsibility for understanding customer needs and working with suppliers to deliver an offering that met their needs, integrating "the 4 Ps"— product, place, price, and promotion—across more than 7,000 stores. It was challenging and fulfilling.

Her subsequent career moves were also exciting, with a series of retail transformations that included C-suite positions as EVP, Omnichannel at Belk, Inc., a leading family-owned department store, and as chief strategy and transformation officer at Southeastern Grocers, a private-equity-owned grocery chain, before ultimately transitioning to what she does today: serving as corporate director and strategic adviser for a portfolio of public and private retail-related companies.

Each of these experiences has been meaningful and has helped her hone her expertise in strategic thinking and the ability to link strategy to operational and organizational change levers, but her most memorable development happened early on while at a global consulting form. Like most professional firms, the company operated using an apprenticeship model, and the typical career path is that you are hired in as an associate and assigned to work on part of a larger client project. If you are successful, you broaden your scope to become the engagement manager, still fully dedicated to just one client at a time but with oversight responsibility for the full project. If you continue to do well, you start to serve multiple clients on multiple projects simultaneously and get involved in business development activities. This is the time when you are given quite a bit of autonomy, although there are a lot of people watching to see how you do while you are in the window for election to the partnership.

Dorlisa had progressed steadily, building her track record with clients in financial services, healthcare, and retail. She had helped introduce a major new client and was serving multiple clients on significant corporate strategy and change efforts, while also taking on industry sector and people leadership roles within the firm. At the time, there had never been a woman partner in the Southeast, and women represented less than 10 percent of the firm's partners worldwide. She was getting regular feedback from both her mentors and an assigned independent evaluator that she was on track for election to the partnership by year's end. But then, the tide changed.

Dorlisa was amid this evaluation window when one of the firm's most senior partners asked her to lead a corporate strategy engagement for his largest client, a manufacturing holding company. Although manufacturing was not an area where she had spent much time, the partner was persuasive, and she did not want to refuse him. She agreed to lead the effort despite her reservations about the client and the industry not being a great fit, but she was determined to do all that she could to help and valued the opportunity to work with him.

The CEO had decided that the company needed a new strategy. It had been operating as a financial holding company with a portfolio of independent business units (each served by its own separate partner). Given changes in the industry, the CEO saw a need to achieve greater synergy across the businesses. The project was focused on defining the top-down corporate strategy and critically assessing each business unit's fit with the new direction. The problem was that the CEO had not taken the time to gain buy-in from the business unit leaders. They, along with the partners who served them, resisted the new direction. They were not bought in on even the *need* for a corporate strategy much less one that could reduce their power.

Their resistance impacted Dorlisa when, during the meeting to finalize the fall slate of election candidates, several of her colleagues questioned whether she should have stood up to the senior partner and forced him to redirect or stop the project. Unaware of the noise, Dorlisa felt that she was still on track for partner, but just as she was leaving town for a training, she was blindsided with a call that explained that the local partnership was pulling her out of the running for election that fall. They were not even going to submit her as a candidate. Dorlisa was shocked.

She went home to talk to her husband, a trusted source of strength and a good sounding board, to give herself time to think. Dorlisa decided to treat the situation like one of her projects at the firm. She would do an in-depth analysis of the situation, try to separate her emotions, and figure out what happened. She canceled her training trip and started a series of interviews internally to gain understanding, do an honest analysis and figure out what this meant for her prospects as a partner.

After her self-analysis, she realized that her supporters were in fact trying to protect her opportunity to make partner by pulling her out of the running so the noise would not confuse her otherwise strong case. That did not take away the sting, but it at least helped her see good intent. She also learned that some of the noise was around her more reserved leadership style and personality. The partners serving the manufacturing divisions who had more limited exposure to her were questioning whether she was tough enough for the partnership role. Given the lack of women partners, they were accustomed to a more aggressive, take charge male style.

She also gained some self-awareness during this process. She had taken the Myers-Briggs Type Indicator® and confirmed that her personality type was INTJ. This type is often called the architect, and she is true to type. She is an introverted thinker and problem solver. At the consulting firm, she had been great at analysis but needed to be more extraverted and more directive versus consultative at times. The firm provided her with a coach, and she worked on varying her style and decided to stay with and prove that she could make it to partner. However, she was going to do it on her own terms. She transitioned out of the manufacturing assignment and doubled down on financial services.

Throughout her consulting career, Dorlisa had three stand-out mentors/sponsors. One played a critical role during this period by recommending her to the managing director in Australia who was seeking help with a competitive negotiation for a new financial services client. She helped win the client and committed to go there to lead the first phase of the engagement. The conventional thinking was that she should stay local while proving her readiness for partner. But she lives by the mantra that you should do the things that you will most regret later if you don't. So, she defied local partner wisdom and went on the big Qantas plane to Australia for several months. There the managing director entrusted her with leading the strategy effort and relationship with the new CEO.

Her strategy skills and increased self-confidence were the perfect combination for success, and she excelled with the freedom to lead her own way. The Australian senior partner became a strong vocal advocate to her partners back home in the US. He told them that she was already doing everything that partners do, and she was doing it well. He was influential in Dorlisa being formally put up for election in the next cycle. Having been told that her setback might cost her a year or more, she was elected partner within six months.

This career setback was a painful time in Dorlisa's career, but she became stronger by taking more control of her life and being less afraid of what would happen. She chose to do the thing she wanted and would remember as a great life experience over the recommended path. She is thankful for the mentors and especially for those who went beyond mentoring to pull her into positions that stretched her skills. Both her consulting and corporate experience are helpful today as she operates as a strategic adviser and corporate director to multiple public and private companies. Her career has been quite a journey, and Dorlisa is satisfied that she did not miss the good stuff.

Words of Wisdom from Dorlisa to You

- At major fork in the road, ask yourself what you will most regret NOT doing later in your life. Take that path—even if the outcome is uncertain—you will still be glad you traveled down it.
- Be intentional in sustaining relationships through the years. You tend to lose track of people if you are not intentional. Really protect and nourish your relationships.
- If you are an introvert, try to find the right balance of time to rejuvenate and the times when it is best for you to stay with the group and be engaged. If you always default to stepping back to regain your energy, you will miss important discussions and decisions that may get made over dinner and drinks instead of in the conference room.
- When a situation changes, be quick to take stock. Figure out where the situation stands and what your options are. Keep in mind that everyone impacted may be under a lot of stress. You have to work the problem from both angles, people, and solutions.
- Place high value on your ability to work under uncertainty. Treat changing situations like puzzles to solve.
- Ultimately it helps to be an optimist. Go into every situation believing that you can make it better.

Sonja Vodusek

Managing Director, The Peninsula
London Hotel and Residences
Location: London, England, United
Kingdom

My Highest Achievements

1. Lived and worked in 13 destinations in 7 countries: Australia, Ireland, Japan, Czech Republic, United States, Philippines, and United Kingdom
2. First female general manager ever appointed to a luxury hotel in Japan
3. Led deep cultural change at The Peninsula Tokyo and achieved significant results in developing people, product, and profit; outside of the flagship hotel in Hong Kong, drove the best financial results in the hotel's 10-year history

Stumbling Blocks or Stepping-Stones

Sonja's appointment to the position of managing director at The Peninsula London was the culmination of decades of progress within her chosen career as an international hotelier. This path started in Australia, where Sonja grew up. As a young girl, she learned about business by working with her family's company. Her parents were Slovenian immigrants who came to Australia and settled in a small rural community. Sonja learned the value of hard work and commitment from an early age. During her high school years and for a short time after, she contributed to the family business by handling the finances and industrial relations. One valuable lesson came from her father, who taught her to be approachable and accessible. He dedicated time with their employees, and his kindness, generosity, honesty, and transparency were all traits that Sonja would one day adopt herself as she navigated a range of leadership positions.

Sonja knew she wanted to make her own mark on the world, beyond the family business. Inspired by a magazine article about a Swiss hotel-management school opening in Sydney, she made up her mind to attend the Blue Mountains International Hotel Management School, and there began her career in hospitality.

After completing hotel management school, Sonja started on the front lines in housekeeping, as a maid cleaning hotel rooms in Japan. The work was tough and the hours were long, but like many top hoteliers, knowing the business from the bottom up and appreciating the importance of every member of the team proved invaluable. Sonja soon rose up the ladder and began managing others, with her father's voice always in her head reminding her that wherever she worked she should run it like it's her own business. She should take charge and avoid making make excuses, because she owns it. He told her to do what's right, put the people first, and he ensured her that if she did these things, the profits would follow.

As Sonja's responsibilities and achievements grew, management noticed. They gave her more staff to lead and began to send her to other locations to work. Relishing the opportunity to live and work in many cities around the world, Sonja moved to Sydney, Melbourne, Dublin, Tokyo, Houston, Prague, Manila, New York, and Washington, DC. Today, she can't say which was her favorite, because each city became a part of her and added depth to her life and career. In one city she was promoted. In another she fell in love. Sonja learned more about herself and more about other people in every location. Her life has always been long on experiences but short on work-life balance, as the hotel business requires commitment to extensive hours and always-available leadership.

There were struggles along the way. Early in Sonja's career, she accepted a role in a hotel where she was tasked to raise the standards. Unfortunately, she wasn't well received within the existing team. It was challenging to instill shared values and manage strong personalities who felt the need to undermine new leadership ideas. On occasion, the whole experience felt overwhelmingly difficult, but Sonja was determined to commit to 12 months, marking off the days on her calendar. The dedication proved invaluable, and during this role, Sonja worked closely with the HR division and learned to adjust her leadership style to achieve results. The only thing she refused to compromise on were her standards.

When the year was up, there was a silver lining. The many hours spent with the HR office created an unexpected friendship. The HR director became a mentor and then a good friend. Today, some 25 years later, she continues to mentor Sonja and works with her leadership teams around the world.

Later in her career, Sonja encountered a similar situation, but with more maturity and the help of a coach, she was able to resolve it swiftly. Like many leaders in business, there is a lot of learning to be done along the way. A vital tip is to sit down, one-on-one, and have a discussion with team members when there is a problem. Never assume they realize the impact of their behavior, but take the time to explain and listen.

One of the greatest lessons learned is that just because the culture that you work in speaks the same language as you, it does not mean that the culture is the same. Leadership styles need to fit in with the cultural context to be effective. Now a seasoned hotelier, Sonja understands every part of the hotel business and is able to tap all the management and leadership skills learned on her journey, none greater than those she learned from her family back in Australia.

Words of Wisdom from Sonja to You

- Trust your instincts: believe in yourself and do not be swayed into doing something you do not want to do.
- Be kind to yourself and patient with others.
- Find a mentor, someone you respect and who will always tell you the truth, because the more senior you become, the more yes people you will have around. You cannot do it alone.
- It is important to work out your ultimate purpose and vision. Spend time thinking about your personal objectives and why you are doing what you do.
- There is light at the end of the tunnel, but why not get in the tunnel and light it yourself? Get to know people outside of your own industry to get a wider perspective.
- Do things that get you out of your comfort zone.
- Pay it forward: guide others and share your experience generously.
- Ask yourself: how do I stay relevant in such an ever-changing world? Leadership is a never-ending learning journey.

Facing Giants and Coming Out Stronger

JEANINE CHARLTON

SVP, Chief Technology and Digital
Officer at Merchants Fleet
Location: Greater Chicago Area,
Illinois, United States

MY HIGHEST ACHIEVEMENTS

1. Named SVP, Chief Technology Officer and Digital Officer for Merchants Fleet
2. Received CIO of the Year Orbie Award 2020 corporate finalist; advisory board member, awards chair 2021
3. Appointed to the National Diversity Council Top 50 Most Powerful Women in Tech in 2020

STUMBLING BLOCKS OR STEPPING-STONES

Some people get more than their share of challenges in this life, and Jeanine Charlton is one. You can see it in the depth in her eyes and the strength in her words. She is a successful leader and parent who spends her energy thinking about others, what they need and how they can learn, grow, and add their voice to the world. She has always focused on learning and growing herself, but it took a little fate to get her on the career path that has catapulted her to being one of the top women in tech.

Born and raised in Michigan, Jeanine started working at 13 and never stopped. Her grandparents were immigrants from Europe, and she can remember times when her father had to work three jobs at the same time just to pay the bills. Neither of her parents was college educated, but they knew hard work, and they supported Jeanine in every way they could even though they couldn't help financially. She went to Central Michigan University, but she didn't get the luxury of having a lot of fun, because she had to work through college.

She didn't know what to major in or what she wanted to do with her life, so when she ended up working for a law firm as an office manager and found the work interesting, she thought she would likely finish college and go to law school; but fate stepped in. She heard that General Motors had acquired Electronic Data Systems, and they were hiring a lot of people. At the encouragement of a friend, she walked into the recruiting office without an appointment. They told her to come back the next day, and when she did, they hired her on the spot. That was the first step on her tech path. She started out in human resources, but once she got in the door she demonstrated her leadership skills, learned aggressively, and progressed quickly. The culture was *work hard and you will be rewarded*, and that fit Jeanine perfectly. She had mentors who helped her, but she also thrived in the challenging, fast-paced environment.

She had no technical background, but when she was asked to take a role leading technology and running her first profit and loss line, she took it. She learned to be a really good leader, and that made up for what she didn't know in technology. She used her leadership skills to build and grow strong technical teams. It also helped her realize that career paths have no set way that they must be done. You can get there from a variety of directions. Though under different corporate names due to acquisitions, she stayed with the company just over 30 years.

Her last assignment ended up being a spinoff, and it was here that she began to seek a seat on a corporate board. While meeting with

Brendan Keegan, VelocityHub CEO, who had become a friend and mentor, she asked for a little advice on finding her first board. He gave her some advice, but he did even more. A week went by, and then he called and asked if Jeanine would consider interviewing for a seat on the board where he also served, at Merchant's Fleet. She said yes and was soon a board member. This became an important pivot in Jeanine's career, as Brendan went from being a mentor to a champion who actively helped her get a board seat; it's a good reminder of how we can all be both mentors and champions for others.

Jeanine hadn't been there three months before the board convinced Brendan to join the company as the CEO, which he accepted. And then it didn't take him long to pursue Jeanine as the company's chief technology and digital officer, and this is where her years and years of work and success have culminated in quite a lot of recognition in recent months.

She doesn't brag about it, because that's not her style. She's fairly private, and because of that, when challenges come, most people never know. They did come, hard and fast. Midcareer, when her children were 14 and 15, Jeanine found herself needing to make a change. Her husband had become an alcoholic, and while she had done all that she knew to help him pull out of it, nothing had worked. It was no longer a safe and conducive home to raise her children. She needed to leave the marriage of 23 years, and at the same time she had been asked by her company to relocate from Michigan to Virginia. It was a lot to deal with at once, but she thought it would help to have a new start for herself and for her children. But everything took a turn for the worse, when not one but both of her kids were diagnosed with Lyme disease and became very sick.

Lyme disease is brought on by a bite from a deer tick typically found in a wooded or grassy area. The diagnosis and treatment process can take years. Before the battle with Lyme disease was over, Jeanine's daughter had missed two years of high school and had a very invasive nasal surgery, as the disease had settled into her nasal cavity. Her son missed his entire high school experience, had his gallbladder removed, and his appendix burst. Both ended up in homeschool during this time.

Eventually, they fully recovered and have gone on to have happy, successful lives, and both have a mental strength well beyond their years.

It's been a long journey, but Jeanine relied on her faith to get them through. She also had family come and help when they could, but ultimately she just knew that failure was not an option. She didn't have the time or energy to focus on her own struggles. She had to be successful at the job because there was no one else to put food on the table and she had to get her children through this crisis. They were battling their own challenges. Their parents were divorced; their dad was an alcoholic; they were in a new state with limited ability to meet friends, and they were in excruciating pain. Jeanine had to be their beacon of hope and light. She had to set the right example. She had to make it okay for her children. The silver lining is that the three of them grew extremely close. They become a tight-knit team with a bond of strength between them. They know they can handle whatever challenges they face, as individuals and as a family. And another silver lining is that their dad eventually conquered his addiction and has been sober for many years, with a positive relationship with both his kids and Jeanine.

Jeanine managed to survive this extremely difficult period, and her company, which provides fleet vehicles to the nation's top companies, will deliver millions of packages this year. This represents incredible growth, due to the pandemic and its impact on buying patterns. It's been quite a journey, and perhaps the best days are still in front of her.

WORDS OF WISDOM FROM JEANINE TO YOU

- If you're in a relationship with an addict, be kind to yourself and just know that it's not your fault and that you are not responsible for what that particular individual is doing in the situation that they're in. You can't fix it. I know it's hard when you love somebody, and you want to see them get well. But when you get to the point where their repeated behavior is potentially harmful or is having a negative impact on you and your family, you have a responsibility to make sure that you and your family are going to be safe and okay.

- I also encourage every professional to learn continuously and to keep your skills current.
- Work your network, read, and learn. If you find yourself not learning new skills, then it's probably a time to step back and reflect upon that, because we live in a world that is constantly changing. We have to pivot and adapt very quickly, and I think we've proven that we can.

ELAINE DORWARD-KING

Non Executive Director
Location: Park City, Utah, United States

MY HIGHEST ACHIEVEMENTS

1. Leading multi-stakeholder engagement over one year which in 2016 led to a landmark, landscape-level conservation agreement in Nevada—the Sage Brush Ecosystem Conservation Agreement between Newmont Mining Corporation, US Department of Interior and State of Nevada—encompassing 1.4 million acres of land on which biodiversity would be protected or enhanced while allowing multiple land uses, including hunting, ranching, and mining

2. Leading Richards Bay Minerals, in South Africa, as managing director from 2011 to 2013, achieving top-tier financial and production results, improving safety results with no fatalities, and leading cultural transformation in workforce

3. Being part of leadership teams that developed and implemented global, world-class standards for health, safety, and environment (HSE) in the mining industry, changing industry understanding and commitment to HSE and improving performance

70 percent or more over a decade, and being part of the greater mining industry contribution to sustainable development in communities impacted by operations

STUMBLING BLOCKS OR STEPPING-STONES

Elaine Dorward-King grew up in rural East Tennessee in the foothills of the Great Smoky Mountains, a beautiful area known for its four distinct seasons. They have mountains for the winter, vibrant awakenings in the spring, lakes and warmth in the summer, and when the leaves change in the fall it is so dramatic it seems a little mystical. Growing up, Elaine and her family always had something on the agenda for outdoor exploration, whether it was hiking, fishing, canoeing, or camping. There was always something to do, and Elaine fell in love with the outdoors at an early age. When she started thinking about what she wanted to do for a career, she knew she wanted to work in the environment; but at that time, role models were few and she didn't know of any careers that seemed suitable. So, she decided that being a physician would be a good and respectable career.

She went to Maryville College in Tennessee for her undergraduate degree in chemistry. While she was there, through the mentoring and support of several faculty members, she realized that she could become an environmental scientist and work on problems like water and land contamination, conservation, and preservation. She was sold on that idea immediately, and when she finished at Maryville, she went to Colorado State University to get a PhD in chemistry focusing on becoming an environmental scientist.

After completing her doctorate, Elaine accepted a position with Monsanto, a massive and integrated chemicals and agricultural company headquartered in St. Louis, Missouri. Her initial job was in agricultural sciences working in biotechnology. It was a great place to launch her career. They provided extensive training and education as well as stretch assignments such as taking on supervisory responsibilities early in her career, leading teams, and the like. She also benefited from two supervisors who advocated for her rapid advancement. She ended up staying at Monsanto for seven years, but St. Louis was nothing like the Smoky Mountains or the Rocky Mountains, and the outdoor lifestyle she desired took precedence over career. She and her husband at the time decided to move to the Pacific Northwest, where she had landed a job with a consulting firm in Seattle, Washington.

There she was able to focus on environmental issues and problem-solving. Overall compensation was less, but she didn't care. Seattle is a beautiful part of the world and she wanted to go there, so she and her husband packed up dogs, bicycles, and canoes and headed west. They loved living in Seattle, and the work was interesting, but it wasn't perfect. She wanted to lead change and see it through, and she was thinking about this when a search firm called trying to recruit her for a position with Kennecott Corporation, a mining company owned by Rio Tinto Group and located in the greater Salt Lake City area.

After the third call and a glimpse of the role description, Elaine agreed to have a conversation. She went to Utah and found the Kennecott leaders to be very impressive. They wanted to hire Elaine to do something she knew she would be passionate about, using a scientific approach to guide decisions regarding environmental cleanup of historic mining waste, working on both ecological and human health aspects. Elaine accepted and moved to Park City, Utah, where her career with Kennecott and Rio Tinto began to take off.

After a short time, Elaine transitioned to an environmental manage-ment role that broadened her responsibilities and experience, including taking on consideration of product-stewardship issues regarding copper. In this work, the focus was on the toxicology of copper materials for both human health and the environment. She represented Kennecott and Rio Tinto at the International Copper Association, where research regard-ing the impacts of copper on the human body and physiology as well as in the environment was being sponsored. She passionately worked to convince the industry that this was work worth supporting, and her advocacy caught the attention of executives in the Rio Tinto headquarters, in London.

Soon, they offered her a position in the United Kingdom, working as an environmental scientist. Here, she focused on gold instead of copper, which turned out to be an exciting change. To get to the gold mines, she traveled the world and visited places she never would have dreamed she would go, including Indonesia, Papua New Guinea, most parts of Australia, and some parts of South America. It was a great experience.

After two years, she had the opportunity to come back to the United States to work for Rio Tinto Borax, where she continued to grow and expand her skill set, adding health and safety as well as regulatory affairs to her role. After several years at Rio Tinto Borax, the leaders in London called Elaine, and this time the offer was big. She would be leading global health, safety, and environment (HSE) for all of Rio Tinto. It was a huge job, with Rio Tinto being one of the first in the industry to drive global standards for HSE performance throughout the organization. Elaine led development of the standards and then, with her team, supported the operational leaders in implementation.

Her crowning achievement at Rio Tinto was her last. She was offered the managing director role for Richards Bay Minerals in South Africa. That made Elaine the business unit leader for one of the world's largest producers of titanium dioxide feed stock as well as other related metals. She was responsible for the profit and loss and about 4,000 employees and contractors. This was an integrated sand dune mining, mineral processing, and smelting operation in rural Kwa Zulu Natal. As the business leader, Elaine learned how to build community and government relations beyond what she had ever done in her other roles. She had to use every skill she had learned and learn many new ones to ensure that she ran the business at a high-performance level while ensuring a positive social impact with a diverse mix of stakeholders.

After twenty years with Rio Tinto and at the request of a long-term colleague, Elaine spent the next six and a half years as the executive vice president for sustainability and external relations at Newmont Mining

Corporation, the largest gold mining company in the world. Once she left, she was quickly scooped up by several corporate boards where she strives to contribute to positive social and environmental impact throughout the world.

Her career has been exemplary, but there were many challenges all along the way. One that stands out was an unexpected political play inside a company for which Elaine worked. She was leading an integrated function for health, safety, and environment. There were some changes that were occurring inside the company with a goal to make the company stronger and improve the operating model. Elaine was on board with improvements but blindsided when a proposal was put forward to change her portfolio and break apart what she had spent at least five years putting together.

When she was informed, her first reaction was to say, "No, that's not the right thing for the company." There could have been a powerplay on the other side of this scenario, but that wasn't what Elaine was thinking about. She knew, deep down, that the best risk mitigation for the company was in the design she had led, but she's a scientist, so she went away and thought about it. She thought through the arguments being made for breaking it apart and tried to look objectively at the options. Settled in her own mind that her initial response was correct and the way it stood was better than the proposed breakup, she asked a trusted colleague about how to approach the issue.

She went back to the team working on the restructure and proposed an objective third-party study with external benchmarking against companies that were recognized as leaders in these areas and an internal survey of leaders and employees. The objective was to collect information to determine the most appropriate way to organize that part of the business. Then she used her long-term, trusted network and found an executive at the most senior level of the company to sponsor the work instead of doing it herself. It was hard to argue with that approach, and they conducted the study. They learned that there is no one right way to organize a company, but the research indicated that the path they were on was the one most likely to achieve their desired results and that the support from inside the organization for keeping things the way they were was strong. The powerplay was squashed.

Elaine has always been a strategic thinker, and she was very strategic during this struggle. As she thinks back about how she was able to come through it successfully, she notes that she benefited from having sponsors, advocates at the executive level, and aligned peers across the organization who were as influential as those who were suggesting the change. She took time to do some deep thinking, analysis, and reflection before making any moves and talked it over with a trusted adviser. At the end of the day the combination of strong advocates supporting her position and objective data to back it up won the argument.

Words of Wisdom from Elaine to You

- Before you get there, make sure you have a strong network in your organization, including above you, below you, and, critically, parallel to you.
- When you get there, make sure your motivations are clear to you and others, that you are true to your values, all about what is best for the organization and not just about your own career.

Arti Singh

CEO, Breakthrough Improvement Now
Location: Orlando, Florida, United States

My Highest Achievements

1. Founded a consulting firm, advising over 10 Fortune 500 companies
2. Attained the level of a senior vice president at a Fortune 25 company, Bank of America; the only diverse woman in the Global Wealth and Investment Management President's circle
3. Reimagined business development process, increasing sales productivity resulting in a revenue lift of $520 million

Stumbling Blocks or Stepping-Stones

Arti Singh is a leader who gets things done. There is a saying that the busiest people do the most, and that fits Arti perfectly. Her schedule may be full, but if she encounters a job that needs to be done, she will lead it, assign it, or do it herself. She is straightforward with a very agreeable delivery style. She could probably share difficult feedback in a meeting inviting open discussion, and later all parties would feel that they are at a better place, because her delivery style is so nonconfrontational. She doesn't usually have to share difficult news as she is hired by Fortune 500 companies to come in and build value by transforming businesses, streamlining complex processes, mitigating risks, enhancing supply chains, and integrating companies' post-mergers and acquisitions. The leaders in these companies already know they have problems, so when Arti shows up with solutions, they are happy to hear what she has to say.

Arti is a first-generation Indian American. Her parents, Dr. Mahendra and Krishna Singh, moved to the United States from Delhi, India, in the late 1950s. Arti was their first child to be born as an American. Her father was a professor and her mother a school principal in India, and they came to the US to further their education and pursue the American dream. They arrived in West Lafayette, Indiana, home of Purdue University, where Dr. Singh, her father, attained a PhD in physics and her mother pursued her master's degree. During this time, there was not as much diversity in the Midwest as found on the coasts. Arti felt it immediately, as the only Indian student from the time she began nursery school and throughout her entire public-school education in the Chicago and Boston suburbs. She learned early on that she was different, in that there was a different language spoken at home. Her family ate different foods, celebrated different holidays, and her mother dressed differently than others. She worked to find ways to fit in and rarely drew attention to herself in an out-of-the-norm way.

Even though she worked to fit in, Arti was proud of her heritage and extremely proud of her parents. They were both intelligent professionals, but English was their second language, and if things didn't come out quite right, Arti was quick to their defense. When she moved to Boston, the issue of diversity faded into the background, as there was a larger melting pot where people were more accepting of and interested in learning about cultural differences.

Arti felt fortunate to live in a city with such great educational opportunities. She attended Tufts University for her bachelor's degree in economics and healthcare policy, and Boston University for her MBA. She originally planned to go into marketing, but during grad school, she had found that her Harvard-experienced professor Bob Leone consistently called on her in his case-study-style course. In her diligent preparation for his classes, she credits him for opening her eyes to Operational Excellence and Lean Six Sigma as an area of great interest, which turned into a lifelong passion and career.

Originally fascinated by the healthcare industry, she worked at Harvard Pilgrim Health Care. She dedicated 10 years to quality improvement at the large HMO, and during that time she began to do the most natural thing for her. She began to find areas that needed improvement and then set about getting it done. She increased patient access, improved staff productivity, brought new products to market faster and more frequently; but at the 10-year mark, Arti began to worry about getting pigeonholed in an industry, so she decided it was time to make a change.

She then moved into finance and banking. When Arti began her first job in finance, she soon had déjà vu. Her field of expertise is known as operational excellence with an origin in industrial engineering principles. This is a male-dominated profession. When she moved into banking and finance, she realized this, too, was a male-dominated industry. So, when the expertise and industry came together, she was often the only diverse person and the only woman in the room. Her early years coming back to her, she thought about how to fit in and learned to maneuver through the old-boys' network.

Arti knew she could figure out how to fit in beyond just being a coworker. She wanted to be seen as part of the team and one of the guys. She wanted to establish trust and friendships that would help as they worked together to achieve company goals. Having a genuine interest in sports and knowing that this could be one way to have non-work discussions, so she would make sure she was on top of the final scores and key plays for the local sports teams over the weekend so that she could chime in on Monday mornings. If the guys went out for a beer after work, she would join them. She took the time to develop relationships and friendships. She didn't want her colleagues to look at her as a competitor, a woman, or a diverse person. She wanted them to look at her as a teammate. Her efforts along with her approachable personality helped and Arti was able to build credibility and over time become a trusted member of the team, but the whole process had to be repeated each time she changed companies.

Arti eventually made her way back to healthcare, taking executive-level roles at CVS Health, and continued to Charles River Laboratories before starting her own firm where she brings her operational excellence and expertise to companies like Coca-Cola, Oracle, Staples, and others. In addition, she serves as board member and board adviser on multiple boards. Her career and reputation are now well established, but facing the male-dominated finance world, on top of her male-dominated profession, was one of her most trying seasons.

During the most difficult periods of adjustment, to relieve stress she relied on physical exercise, eating well, and her best friend, Lesa Stramondo Botti, who is an attorney. Lesa helped her sort through what was happening from an outside perspective, ensuring Arti that her experience was not abnormal and that she was new and they all had known one another for much longer.

Later, Arti joined an all-women's professional organization called The Boston Club. It has over 700 professional executive women, many of whom had gone through similar struggles. There was a whole other level of understanding, support, and advice, because Arti could not only talk to other professional women, but she could also find one or more women who were SVPs in banking or finance, so the relatability rose exponentially. She is still a member of The Boston Club today and serves on the governance committee.

Networks can be a powerful place of camaraderie and helpfulness. The members of Arti's networks share their expertise, contacts, and support, offering a place to land where members can reveal who they really are, pick each other up when they need it, and become better by sharing and learning from one another. There is also a strength for the members that comes from knowing they are not alone, that they can go forward with all the fierceness and drive they have inside of them, to compete, to win, to fail, and to know that the network is there on the good days and the bad days. There is always someone to lend a hand or toast a success. Networks are a source of community and strength.

Words of Wisdom from Arti to You

- Build a strong network, and find people outside of your work environment, like a professional women's organization. Nurture those relationships, offer them support, and pay it forward!
- Confide in your best friend, someone you can trust and has your best interests in mind.
- Take good care of yourself, and that means eating right and working out. There's something in the workout that can be very meditative, just taking in the scenery as you do whatever it is you want to do, whether it's biking, hiking, walking, etc. It centers and balances you.

Life isn't just about work. There is so much more than that: developing teams, nurturing relationships, building networks, and personal growth. Don't forget to value all the aspects that make work fulfilling!

NICOLE PARENT HAUGHEY

Strategic and Data-Driven Chief Operating
Officer
Location: Greater Boston Area,
Massachusetts, United States

MY HIGHEST ACHIEVEMENTS

1. Becoming a respected sell side analyst covering industrial companies without getting an MBA
2. Having the financial and emotional freedom to be able to leave a well-paying, rewarding job with people I loved—at the depth of the financial crisis—to do a startup
3. Becoming a public-company board member soon after identifying it as a goal

STUMBLING BLOCKS OR STEPPING-STONES

Nicole Parent Haughey made her way to the corporate world through sports. She was a small-town, public-school girl from Abington, Massachusetts, who launched what is turning out to be a very impressive career by playing soccer, which led her to Harvard, which led her to Wall Street. She, like many accomplished athletes, is combination of tough and tender. She's mentally tough and strategic, but she's also incredibly passionate, caring, and willing to give whatever she does, with everything she has inside of her. That made her a great athlete, and it makes her a great business leader. As an athlete, Nicole learned to play on a team, drive for performance, review mistakes, receive feedback, and try again. She mastered learning from failures and developed a resiliency to keep getting up and playing no matter how much it hurt, and this bounce-back ability would prove to be an important attribute as she learned to maneuver through the business world.

After earning a bachelor's degree in economics from Harvard, Nicole went to Wall Street, where she picked up the new game she would be playing. Wall Street and athletes go well together, because it is a competitive environment, and if you perform successfully, you will be rewarded. Just like on the soccer field, she had to win more than she lost, learn from her failures, receive feedback, and get back up again and again. She also worked with other high performers and continued to hone her skills at collaboration and working well with others. She did well and made it to managing director at Credit Suisse, where she ultimately oversaw capital-goods research across the US, Europe, and Asia.

While working on some strategic projects around revenue, commissions, and compensation within financial services, Nicole recognized that the industry dynamics were shifting and rapidly creating an opportunity for research analysts to be viewed as revenue producers, not cost centers within an organization.

That shift led to her cofounding an independent equity research firm with a brilliant former boss who taught her what it took to be a great research analyst. Nicole was excited about where her life was going. She had recently been elected "the youngest and first female president of the Harvard Club of New York,"[1] and now she was also going to be a managing partner of the new firm. She and her business partner spent many months working on business plans, but when they created the operating agreement, Nicole was surprised that her partner refused to include a no-nepotism clause. In hindsight, she realized that seemingly trivial detail was an important red flag she missed about their different visions for the company. Her vision was to build a company with an extraordinary culture that disseminated the best industrial research globally.

Eventually she understood that his vision was to build his own legacy, a family-owned-and-run business.

This was Nicole's first business and first partnership, and in the spirit of compromise, she let the no-nepotism clause go, but that proved to be a mistake as he brought in family members to senior and junior roles. She also realized that even though they didn't have other partners in the operating agreement, her business partner's wife and daughter were weighing in heavily on strategy behind the scenes, and their vision was pulling them further and further apart. The stress was already in the business relationship, but when Nicole became engaged and her partner asked if she was still committed to the business, Nicole knew she was done. She responded with one question: "Did you ask that to any of the men who work for us that became engaged while working here?" She knew that he hadn't, so there was no need to wait for an answer. She was angry and ready to move on, but more than anything she felt sad and betrayed. He had been a friend and a mentor, and then he was neither.

Nicole had played hard and experienced a painful loss, but she knew what to do. She bandaged up her injuries and got back on the field. Before long, she was deep in a new game as a senior executive at a Fortune 50 company, where she was one of only two senior women at that level, but this wasn't Wall Street, and she hadn't played this kind of game before. This was a large corporation and laden with internal politics. Winning here was not a clear-cut performance issue. There were all these inter-personal nuances, and Nicole found that there were peers who were trying to undercut her every step of the way. As a person who had a deep understanding of teams, this was like moving to a foreign country. And it was more than that. On top of the one-on-one foul plays with behind-the-scenes sabotage and out-front threats, there was something deeply wrong with the company's culture.

Nicole had stellar performance reviews and was hitting all her performance metrics, so she was completely blindsided when one of her direct reports told her of a rumor that the company was planning to replace Nicole. When she confronted her boss, another longtime mentor who had recruited her to work at the company, he didn't deny it and offered her a different role in the organization. Recognizing it's impossible to lead a team who thinks you are a lame duck, Nicole offered her resignation. However, before she left, there was a coup that resulted in an unexpected change in leadership.

The new CEO asked Nicole to stay on in her old role and report directly to him and help him with the transition. Thinking this would offer a much better scenario, she accepted. Afterward, she assumed that everyone had been told of the change, but she realized that wasn't the case when she found herself in an exit interview with the head of HR. The woman conducting the interview was shocked and seemingly unhappy to learn that Nicole wasn't leaving. Nicole left the meeting, went back to work, and focused on helping the new CEO transition.

Fast-forward to a few months later, and it was Groundhog Day all over again when she was told by another executive that her role and reporting line were changing. She resigned that night with a bruised ego, leaving a lot of money on the table but without the heart to fight about it. She was ultimately replaced by two men who were paid significantly more to do the same job that she had been doing by herself. The mental anguish of back-to-back experiences of betrayal from longtime mentors had taken too much out of her, and she needed to pull back and recover.

It took time, a lot of tears, and some serious self-reflection to get through the grief and clear her head so she could once again play to win. She felt that she had been betrayed twice by people she trusted. She was wounded and paranoid but knew she had to dust herself off, pick herself up, and get back out on the field. She felt the best way to do this was to find a new executive coach with experience in executive transitions. Having been forced to get an executive coach early on in her career to better fit into a newly merged company with two competing cultures, she learned quickly how invaluable an outside perspective can be. Together, Nicole and her new coach worked through Nicole's experiences, where she had missed red flags, and slowly worked to regain her ability to trust her own intuition again. She also surrounded herself with supportive and nurturing people, including her husband, parents, and close friends, who she knew had her back in any situation.

Over time, she owned her role in these situations, understanding where she missed cues and where the responsibility clearly fell on others. She mapped out a plan for her future and knew she had learned some valuable lessons that would help her as she moved forward, namely that life is short and you must be happy in all facets of your life. She used her time between jobs to read, recover, and invest in the next generation of up-and-coming women by starting a program for athletes at her alma mater with an eye toward exposing them to amazing people who are making a difference in the world. The spark in her heart reignited, and she turned her focus again to inspiring others.

Today, Nicole is loving her life and realizes what matters. As chief operating officer for Island Creek Oysters, she chose to join a company with an extraordinary culture that loves high performers but never at the expense of a positive team environment. In a way, she's come full circle and back to the South Shore of Massachusetts where she grew up. She's still settling into to her new role, but this time they are working together as a team, adapting quickly to running a business in a COVID world and thinking about future growth as well as supporting other oyster farmers in their coastal community. She feels like she's on a team again, and together, the team is winning.

WORDS OF WISDOM FROM NICOLE TO YOU

- I am a huge believer in karma; trust that what comes around goes around. That which doesn't kill us only makes us stronger. You will get to the other side of it. It will more than likely be painful, but you'll be so much better off because of it, because these kinds of failures inspire greatness. Remember to laugh and smile along the way!
- Whenever someone you know loses their job, be sure to reach out to them and offer words of encouragement even if you are unsure what the circumstances are or you don't know what to say. Losing a job or being forced to leave one is one of the most humiliating

experiences a successful executive can go through, especially when it's in the public domain. Reach out even if you don't know what to say and share a positive thought or let the individual know how much they've helped you along the way. This is something I learned to do early on and I have forged lifelong friendships as a result of that one kind gesture.

- Be kind to yourself. Don't beat yourself up.
- Invest in yourself; be true to yourself; and make sure that you are also surrounding yourself with supportive people.

---

1. Shapiro, G. (2012, June 18). Harvard Club's New Face. *Wall Street Journal.* https://www.wsj.com/articles/SB10001424052702303703004577472931874791226.

Chapter 5

Vulnerability

"Be kind, for everyone you meet is fighting a hard battle."

— Plato

THE FOLLOWING STORIES HAVE AN underlying theme of *vulnerability*, the act of placing yourself in an emotionally, psychologically, or physically open state where your defenses are down.[1] For leaders, being vulnerable is being authentic, honest, and as transparent as possible.

In the past, many leaders were groomed to have a sort of superhero façade, one that made them look like they didn't have problems; they didn't get tired; and they had all the answers, but times have changed. Today the impression of such an impenetrable exterior isn't needed or desired. We want leaders who can admit they need help and who are accepting of that help when it is offered. We want real, not fake, and if there is something fake going on, it is likely to get outed on social media anyway, so there's no point.

Life's struggles do not stop because you become a leader, and when you have people watching your every move, it's hard to know what to do when you are at your most vulnerable moments. In the stories that follow, you will see leaders with stories of vulnerability to the core, their pain, and their grace fully exposed. We hope that you don't have to go through such experiences, but if you do, these stories may give you some hope to get through and some wisdom on how to do it.

161

IRAM SHAH

Adviser to CEOs and Boards
Location: Greater Chicago Area, Illinois,
United States

MY HIGHEST ACHIEVEMENTS

1. Leading the digital transformation as a SVP at Schneider Electric, a $6 billion North American business, via customer experience, digital tools/application, data analytics and AI, resulting in 16 percent increase in customer satisfaction, customer care revenue increasing by 200 percent in less than two years

2. Managing a global career in Fortune 100 companies in four diverse industries across five countries

3. Working with different cultures and in different industries, helped me better understand the levers of success in any business and developed more insight into human condition at work place. This helped me to become a better leader.

STUMBLING BLOCKS OR STEPPING-STONES

Born in Peshawar, Pakistan, Iram Shah's journey has been filled with mountains beyond mountains of incredible scenery and experiences as well as the challenging and, at times, almost impossible terrain. Her father came from a small village called Kangra, north of Peshawar, where girls still have difficulty going to school. They often marry as early as 14 to 16 and live second-class lives with no freedom or empowerment. Until recently, this area was a hub for extremists who destroyed schools and shot girls to prevent them from going to school. Nobel Peace Prize winner Malala Yousafzai was one of them.

Iram's parents left Kangra and moved to Peshawar, where Iram grew up. It was a very conservative society laden with tradition and role expectation, but her father was broad-minded and made sure that she was educated and empowered to do whatever she wanted to do. And, unlike many of the other men in town, he encouraged her not to let gender get in the way of her dreams. He told her to act like a woman but think like a man, because in the world at the time, the rules were made by men.

There were two acceptable career roles for women in her region: education and medicine, but she took her father's advice and decided she wanted to be a businesswoman, not an assistant to a leader but a leader herself. Her parents were taken aback. It was quite a discussion, but Iram reminded her father of his guidance through the years and ultimately won the approval and the support of both parents. However, her challenges were just beginning.

There was one—only one—commerce college and not a single woman in attendance. Iram went anyway. She entered as the only girl in a class of 80 boys. At the professor's inquiry of future plans, she let him and the other students know that she intended to go to the United States to get an MBA from Harvard. They all laughed, but she did it anyway.

Today, she has completed the Advanced Management Program at Harvard Business School, and she did in fact become a businesswoman. She has worked for Fortune 100 companies in five countries, across four diverse industries, including consumer goods, oil and gas, finance, manufacturing, energy management, and automation. She has helped develop some of the world's best-known brands, including Gatorade and Coca Cola, and held C-suite positions in well-known companies, including Schneider Electric, Zurich Financial, and British Petroleum.

Her achievements in business are amazing, but there is so much more to Iram than her work. She cares deeply for her friends and family. She takes leadership seriously and works hard to help others, personally and professionally. Her identity is not a job. Her identity is tied into her life's purpose, which became clear through the most unexpected tragedy.

Iram's career had taken her to Zurich, Switzerland, where she was group head of marketing and planning for Zurich Insurance Company Ltd. Her husband, Mahmood, has always supported her work and gave preference to her career over his own, so he and their daughter, Sonia, relocated with Iram. All was going well. They had a good life. Iram had a great career. Sonia traveled the world with her and was growing into an amazing young woman. She was not like most of the girls her age. Sonia loved reading and listening to music and almost never asked for anything for herself. She spoke five languages and wanted to make a difference for others.

But then suddenly, Sonia was gone. She died in a car accident at the age of 18. Her death shook Iram to the core. Numb at first, she could not cry. She could not function. She just could not believe Sonia was gone. She had to take a step back and try to figure out what all of this meant. Life had been going along without too much reflection, and then it was all reflection. She had a friend tell her that she needed to take action and turn her tragedy into something meaningful. She could stay in her room and cry and become lost in her grief, or she could do something with all of this, something for good.

That is when Iram started to move again. She took time to reevaluate herself both personally and professionally, and she knew that her life had to have purpose. Professionally, her work became a passion, a place where she could help transform businesses and make a difference for the people she worked with, but outside of work, there was something else she knew she had to do.

Before the car accident, Sonia had started a mission for educating girls in Pakistan. She graduated from high school a year early and took a gap year. She told her parents that she wanted to go to the village of her grandfather. She felt that the only way she could help was to get to know the girls herself. So she left the comforts, the beauty, and the luxury of Switzerland and traveled to an extremely primitive region in Pakistan. There was hardly any electricity during the day, and the summer days were often 100 degrees Fahrenheit or more. She lived in a very small room in a small village with no running water.

She lived there for a few weeks so she could understand what the girls in that village needed. After she had been there awhile, she called home to Iram and asked for $20,000. Since Sonia did not usually ask for anything, Iram was a little shocked but wanted to hear the rest of the story. Sonia explained that she had learned that one of the main reasons the girls were not going to school was that their parents were afraid to send them out of the village. They need to be able to stay in the village and walk to the school, so Sonia had found some land in the village. She wanted to buy the land and build a school for the girls.

Iram understood. Impressed but without the cash lying around, she decided to say yes anyway, take the money out of her retirement, and send it to her daughter. With that, Sonia founded her mission, bought the land, and started the school. But within a year, she was gone.

Iram decided that she could take Sonia's work and carry it forward. As her friend suggested, she turned her tragedy into something meaningful. Today, the Sonia Shah Organization has a school with 200 children. Seventy-five percent of them are girls. There is also a vocational center for women, and over 200 women have graduated and are now supporting themselves financially.

In addition, getting the girls enrolled in school delays their marriages and subsequent childbirths by several years. Without education, the girls marry so young that childbirth is one of the leading causes of death in young women. This delay in age of childbirth gives their future children a 50 percent greater chance to be healthy and educated. So, these girls that would never have had a chance to read and to write their names, now go to school where they have uniforms provided, computers, a solar system to keep the electricity on, vitamins, and books. There is also water filtration so they can have fresh, clean water. Even though some of them do not even have shoes, the kids come, not walking but running, to the school. Both they and the school are flourishing.

A second pillar for the mission is providing scholarships for girls in the United States. And the third pillar, the Sonia Shah Young Ambassadors, trains and equips this group of dedicated young people to become leaders and make a difference in the world.

There are so many needs, but this is a start. Iram turned the lens around from herself and her own pain to that of others, and she is doing something about it while continuously honoring the life of Sonia.

She still has days when the grief is heavier than others. There are still some pictures that she cannot bare to see, because she does not have the strength. The grief never really goes away, but she does not try to avoid it. The only way through it, is through it. Instead, she takes her grief and acts, just like her friend encouraged her to do, and she uses it to do something good.

WORDS OF WISDOM FROM IRAM TO YOU

- Life is a collection of triumphs and trials. Embrace both and do the best you can. You will not only be remembered for what you achieved and survived but, more important, by the difference you made in other lives.
- Being a leader means being able to see the future that others cannot see and having the courage and insight to translate that vision into an action plan that people can understand, feel part of, and follow. It is about inspiring and influencing others to add value and make a difference.

- There have been many challenges that have shaped my life and career, but losing my teenage daughter shook me to the core and forced me to reevaluate my life both personally and professionally. Personally, it gave my life a purpose, and professionally I became more of a transformational leader with a courage to innovate and help grow and transform businesses. My tragedy is painful but is helping me to become the best version of my true self in all walks of my life.
- You cannot lose hope; always try to learn from your experiences, no matter how painful. A higher purpose to make a difference helped me survive the tragedy. The clarity of purpose distracts me from the pain.
- A sense of higher purpose gave me the guidance.

BHAVANI AMIRTHALINGAM

SVP, Chief Digital Information
Officer at Ameren
Location: St. Louis, Missouri,
United States

MY HIGHEST ACHIEVEMENTS

1. Driving significant technology, enabling business transformations across very large Fortune 500 enterprises (Schneider Electric, Ameren), with a focus on transforming the customer experience while enabling efficiencies across the value chain
2. Working in the technology and energy industry for over 20 years not only managing the internal technology posture but managing customer solutions and innovation in several roles
3. Building high-performing, empowered teams to enable these transformations, by bringing together business and emerging technology skills while balancing the equation around sustained innovation, execution, and effective risk management

STUMBLING BLOCKS OR STEPPING-STONES

Bhavani Amirthalingam lives in St. Louis, Missouri, with her husband and their 17-year-old son and 13-year-old daughter. She is SVP and chief digital information officer at Ameren, a Fortune 500 power company. She was born in Bangalore, India, a city in the heart of the technology industry. She first caught the tech bug at age 12, when computers showed up in school. Bhavani fell in love with the tangible, problem-solving machines and often spent her weekends at the school working on the computers. In India, after the 10th grade, students decide what they will focus on. They choose from math, physics, chemistry, computer science, biology, economics, etc. Bhavani, a bold risk-taker at heart, chose computer science, filled out the paperwork, and took it home to get her parents' signatures, which she suspected might be a challenge, as the industry was very new at the time.

Both of Bhavani's parents have always been supportive of her. Her mother, Banumathi, was a homemaker whose work and focus have always been on family and home. Her father, Amirthalingam, had grown up on a small farm with a large family, and he was the first person to put himself through engineering school. He was very self-driven and self-made, and he continuously told Bhavani that she needed to grow up to be independent. He had seen female relatives become trapped in abusive relationships, and he did everything he could to make sure that his daughter never found herself in that situation. He spent a lot of time doing all he could to train her in every area that he knew would help her to be confident, courageous, and independent. When she was only 6 years old, he told her, "Never let anyone tell you that you can't do something you believe in." These words are now woven into her DNA.

When she was in high school, that statement came in handy as she presented her father with the papers to go into computer science. He did not want to sign them. He told her that computers were fine for a hobby, but he didn't think she could make a career out of it, a phrase she can now tease him about all these years later. But at the time, Bhavani laid out her case over the next few days, and then she gently reminded him of the words he spoke to her as a youth, "never let anyone tell you that you can't do something you believe in." Her closing argument, along with his daughter's bright eyes and wide, dazzling smile, settled the case, and he signed the papers.

Bhavani pursued her bachelor's degree in computer science at the University of Madras in Chennai, Tamil Nadu, India, and through her summer internships learned that she was fascinated by the business side of technology. Afterward, she was accepted into the MBA program at the S.P. Jain Institute of Management & Research, one of the top ten business schools in India. Ninety-eight percent of her classmates were experienced in business, and they became her mentors. She learned tremendously during those two years and put it all to work in her first job as an E-commerce consultant with a startup called Satyam Infoway.

She was there a little over a year before she ended up in a consulting gig in New York City, which eventually led to a job with Sony in the United States and a chance encounter with Karthik Muthusamy, who would eventually become her husband. After they started dating, Karthik had to move to St. Louis to finish his education. The long distance between them was too painful, and they decided to marry, and Bhavani would make the move to St. Louis. She started looking for a position, and soon there were multiple opportunities for her, but one captivated her. While visiting over a weekend, she interviewed at World Wide Technology, on a Sunday.

World Wide Technology was a provider of innovative technology and supply chain solutions with about $500 million at the time. The environment and culture were compelling. They had a great vision, and she liked the cofounders, Dave Steward and Jim Kavanaugh. She followed her heart and took the job. While she was there, they had explosive growth requiring every skill she had and many that she had to learn quickly in her roles as vice president of information technology and later VP of customer solutions and innovation. Today, they are almost $12 billion in annual revenue as well as one of the largest African American–owned companies with most of the Fortune 100 as their customers.

It was during her work at World Wide that Bhavani experienced one of her greatest challenges to date. She was taking on more responsibility and had officially accepted the chief information officer role, and at the same time, she and her husband were starting their family. The job was all consuming, and so was having a newborn. It was hard to catch a breath, much less find any kind of balance. Her husband was always very supportive of her career, but he had a busy career of his own. Bhavani began to have some health challenges.

These were formative years in Bhavani's career as she tried to manage all the competing priorities. She knew her family needed her, and at work she had tremendous responsibilities, and her health issues were not insignificant. A friend stepped in and gave her some advice not to try to do everything herself, that it was too much. Bhavani agreed and began to reach out to others. Her work and family were a great social-support system. Her father moved in for the first two years of her son's life, and both of her parents moved in for two years when her second child was born. Her mother was the one who could calm her down when Bhavani put too much stress on herself, and her husband and friends were always supportive and helpful. Her work and family needed her, and like many leaders, she sometimes lost sight of the need to first take care of herself in order to be able to take care of her family and work!

Even though the CIO role was all consuming and the company was growing like crazy, she had great support and mentorship from Dave and Jim, the chairman and CEO of World Wide. They shaped her in many ways, and she feels very blessed to have worked there. That's why it was an extremely difficult decision when Schneider Electric reached out with a job offer. The job was to be CIO of North American operations for this massive global Fortune 500 company that was publicly traded with over 160,000 employees and $27 billion in revenue. It was a big leap to a complex conglomerate, and if she hadn't loved World Wide so much, the decision would have been easy. She struggled to decide, and when she finally accepted the new position, she felt like she was leaving her family. But there were good things happening at Schneider as well. They had a great passion for transformational change, with digitization at the center of it giving Bhavani a spotlight role in their vision and strategy. Her work there was challenging and fascinating, and from extending her patience to managing her travel, she was stretched in every way.

After a few years, Ameren reached out with another tempting opportunity. Again, the decision was hard, but she would be a part of the leadership team that was transforming the customer experience as well as digitizing and transforming the grid; the bonus was that she would travel less and spend more time with her kids, who were entering their teen years, giving her the opportunity to be more involved in their lives. She made the move.

Bhavani's rise to the top of the house has been laden with rich, rewarding experiences as well as mind-numbing problems and difficulties. Both have brought lessons that she cherishes, including understanding that different seasons in life may require different commitments. Sometimes work needs most of our energy, and sometimes our families need most of our energy. There is no one right way to do it. Each person must figure out what is right for them. And during some of the most difficult seasons, the best thing may be a level of vulnerability and transparency, because often people want to help, but they can't if we don't share that we need their help.

Words of Wisdom from Bhavani to You

- Do not try to figure it out all yourself. Discussing your challenges doesn't make you weak. People will appreciate the transparency and support. Do not create your own ceilings; look out for unconscious and hidden bias.
- Hire people who are smarter than you. That one thing will change your life for the better.
- Don't get too comfortable, and be courageous enough to disrupt yourself, for change is the only thing that is constant.
- Show some empathy. People are going through a lot, so be there for them.
- This is the slowest it's ever going to be. The pace of change is just going to keep accelerating. Decide how you will build the DNA of change, the adaptability inside of you.

Jocelyn Martin-Leano

President, Rushmore Loan Management
Services, Servicing Division
Location: Irvine, California, United States

My Highest Achievements

1. Came to US with one suitcase as a young adult and eventually became president of two companies
2. Built a successful division from 100 to 1,000 employees in eight years, with EBIT margins in the 30 percent range
3. Completed Harvard's Women on Corporate Boards course and admitted to and currently enrolled in Harvard Business School's Advanced Management Program

Stumbling Blocks or Stepping-Stones

Jocelyn came to the United States in her early 20s, as an immigrant with one suitcase. She had a fiery heart and a passion to lead others, but she had to work hard to get positioned for success both before and after her move. She grew up the oldest of four children and a female in a very male-driven society. She chose an unconventional path and went into engineering school in Manila, Philippines, where women made up only about 5 percent of the engineering program. And there was out-and-out gender discrimination in the program at the time. After she received her degree, Jocelyn went to take an engineering test for a job, and midway through the test she was told that only males could apply for the job, a fact omitted from the posting.

But life has many of twists and turns, and she soon immigrated to the United States. There, she found an ad and decided to apply for a position in the mortgage business. She was young, an immigrant, female, and small in stature. And she didn't even know how mortgages worked, as the US had very different processes from those in the Philippines. She had to figure out how to present herself and learn the language. There was much to learn. Then she ended up with her own mortgage, and the lightbulb turned on. She understood how it worked, but she still had to conquer the language barrier and an accent. It wasn't that she didn't know English. She could speak it, read it, and write it, but she just couldn't get the right colloquial vocabulary. Initially, she sounded like a book. But eventually she figured it out, ended up in mortgage banking, and began to climb the ladder.

At Citibank, Jocelyn was asked to help solve a problem: the mortgages were taking too long to close. When someone buys a home, they generally want to be in the home within 60 days. But the bank had some inefficient processes, and her job was to figure it out. She jumped in and used her process engineering background to help solve the problem. She then found her career and has now been in the industry for almost 37 years.

Jocelyn's genuine interest in people was one of the gifts that helped her succeed on her unconventional path. There were lots of people in the industry who were good at the quantitative work and analytical work, but it takes an interest in people to get into a position of leadership. That helped her stand out. Her employees responded to the fact that she genuinely cared about them.

Through the years, Jocelyn stayed in the financial services vertical and worked for several mortgage banks and insurance companies. As she reflects on those transitions, she recognizes the way each experience carried her forward. She took with her new skills, relationships, and knowledge and worked to apply them in her next role. There were supportive bosses who helped her, but everything wasn't easy. And it didn't always work out.

She worked for one company that said it aspired to have a more people-oriented culture. It had plenty of quantitative-analytic types, but it needed something different, something softer. So, they hired Jocelyn, and she brought her people-focused leadership to a COO position. She was good at bringing in different styles and fostering inclusivity, but when the changes started, the company realized that change was very uncomfortable. The company had to stretch in ways that were difficult, and in the end, it didn't work out. The company wasn't ready for the changes that a more people-oriented, inclusive culture required. Jocelyn viewed it as an opportunity to take the experience and pivot.

Despite the setback, she soon landed in a new leadership role, and her successful career path continued. Today, she leads over 1,000 employees across several countries. But at an identifying juncture, her love of leadership went from a career passion to a life purpose, when devastation hit her family. When Jocelyn's two young children were 5 years old and 11 months old, she needed to lead a large systems conversion at work. She went home that evening to see her family and then went back to work for the all-night conversion. When she left, everything was fine. When she returned, her infant son was tossing and turning unexplainably. Within a few hours, he was gone.

Her grief and her guilt for being at work that evening was almost unbearable. She couldn't help but wonder if she could have done more had she been home. Later she would learn that there wasn't anything anyone could have done. Her son's death was caused by a genetic mutation, a thickening of the heart. She didn't know until much later that her two subsequent children also have the gene mutation in their DNA. Her youngest has the same heart condition now and is also autistic.

To this day, Jocelyn must continuously fight the fear that the genetic mutation will take a second child. But fear isn't helpful, so she tried—and still tries—to channel it into something more positive. During that tragic time, she read Rick Warren's book *A Purpose Driven Life*. That gave her some direction, but she also had to adjust her normal mode of operation. Jocelyn is typically self-sufficient. Like many leaders, she finds it hard to ask for help. But when she lost her son, she was facedown, unable to move, and unable to help herself. Yet people came to help, and she had to receive the help. She even had to begin to ask for and accept help, too. She learned that there is no harm in being vulnerable. That was a pivotal point for her, and one that may help many leaders when they go through crushing periods in their life.

With the idea of purpose now solidified in her tragedy, Jocelyn became a more resilient leader. She became unflappable and able to handle any work problem regardless of size, because she now knows that if everyone is still vertical and still breathing, it is a good day. She knows that eventually they will forget the problems of today and not even remember them. And, at the end of the day, it's the people that matter. Tragedy changed her life. It made her a better leader. Leadership became a mission, and she wants to make life better for people.

Words of Wisdom from Jocelyn to You

- Cling to hope. Never, ever give up hope. Keep the faith, and keep persevering. Let your losses define you for good. Cling on to hope at the darkest hour, and never let go.
- You do not become any less of a person or lose any stature if you need some help.
- Relish today, as tomorrow is never guaranteed.
- You may be the smartest person, but if people don't feel good working with you, it's not going to work if you want to be in leadership.
- Prepare thoroughly and work hard. In order to really succeed, you need to do your homework. There is no substitute.

Hana'a AlSyead

Founder and CEO at Wujud
Location: Riyadh, Saudi Arabia

My Highest Achievements

1. Founding Wujud, a social enterprise focused on advancing meaningful and sustainable practices that enhance the economy and benefit society
2. Designing and implementing a system to digitally centralize the operations of Saudi American bank
3. Engineering a methodology to advance diversity in the workplace, focused on gender, which was recognized as a best practice by the World Economic Forum and drafted as a business case study by Harvard Business School

Stumbling Blocks and Stepping-Stones

Hana'a AlSyead's work has taken her from systems engineering to advising world organizations and advocating for full economic integration of women. She is the savvy, straightforward CEO of Wujud, a management consulting firm, think tank, and social enterprise in Saudi Arabia. She founded Wujud with an aspiration of contributing to high-performing economies in which the potential of all humanity is fully explored, enriched, and realized with meaningful impact to societies at large. Hana'a works with clients to help them understand and apply a concept she has developed and refers to as Responsible Business, to change their mindset to be an impact-driven business with a purpose aligned to benefit the economy and society.

Hana'a likes solving problems, but don't worry about pointing them out to her. She's naturally quick to identify order in chaotic situations or areas that need improvement and wastes no time moving into action. She enjoys applying her systems-engineering background and years of experience to help her client organizations solve complex problems as well as shift to positive social impact. Hana'a doesn't accept lip service. She guides organizations to genuinely imbed Responsible Business's concept and tools in their corporate DNA and show it from the inside out. She helps them identify their ultimate purpose and align with it by doing the right thing from the beginning. She has witnessed the benefits and seamless impact of this approach vis-à-vis fixing problems through rework, which can prove to be both a daunting and expensive task.

Hana'a has extensive experience addressing large-scale issues in global organizations. Her early international-university experience in Boston, Massachusetts, was a great beginning to an exciting career.

Hana'a finished high school at 16, and her father, Yousef, decided that the best option for her education was at Simmons, a women's college in Boston, where at that young age she could pursue a degree in computer science, a field not yet offered to women in her country at the time. Yousef believed in his daughter, as he raised his children on par with each other, not differentiating between the boys and girls. He was a proud father, but he was dismayed to learn upon arriving in the US with Hana'a that even though the students were all young women, the professors and the president of the university were men. It was a humorous twist that he accepted, and Hana'a started her university education. It probably helped that he had been educated as a medical doctor and surgeon in Germany and was quite familiar with the Western world and Western education system. By the time Hana'a was ready for graduate school, he had come around to the idea of co-ed universities, and she enrolled in Boston University.

Hana's father was always influential in her way of thinking. Even when she was a young girl, he would point to powerful women like Margaret Thatcher, Prime Minister of the United Kingdom, when she was on television and say, "Women are capable of doing a great job in anything they set their minds to do." As a result, Hana'a has always had aspirations for great achievements and was never burdened with small thinking or imposed limitations. She applied her engineering skills and results-oriented thinking to projects at the Saudi American Bank, United Saudi Bank, and Olayan Financing Company. She was on a success fast track when her father passed away and took the wind from Hana'a's sails. She hadn't even realized the extent to which a desire to please her father had fueled her drive—to make him proud by showing him more of the great things she could achieve—just as he had encouraged her to do when she was young. Without him to share the success with, her accomplishments meant less and felt ordinary.

It took a lot of personal work to get through this period. Hana'a started journaling, to process her emotions, feelings, and thoughts after losing her father. At first, it was just a way to carry her through her grief, but something else was happening too. She was honing her writing skills that she hadn't thought much about until this time. As a child, she had enjoyed writing short stories and poetry. After she lost her father, her journaling helped her take her dormant skill further, and her journals evolved. She kept writing stories from her childhood memories, some of which are suitable for young adults, until she ended up completing a memoir about her father that blossomed into a memoir about herself, him, and every person in Hana'a's life that she loved who left a mark on her being and who was now gone. It was an important time and process that turned into something beautiful as she worked out her grief and shared her love and life lessons on paper.

Words of Wisdom from Hana'a to You

- I believe in leadership but not in the way we are told—that it has to be from the front. Leadership can be in front, to show the way and give direction; from the middle, to motivate and keep the momentum and/or even from the back, where no one is left behind.
- Being straightforward, to the point, and factual is who I am. Throughout my career, I witnessed people feeling challenged by these traits and prefer to keep a safe distance from them. It is in this safe distance that new realities come to life, which I now refer to as politics.
- Don't be afraid of starting over. Sometimes, you have to dismantle things and then put them back together in a new way. What you re-create will always advance your growth.
- And finally, do your best to do the right thing, right from the first time. There is an inherent reward (and blessings) in doing good and doing it the best way you can. You will know what is right once you are clear on and aligned with your highest purpose.

Laying Down a High-Level Position for the Love of Another

PATRICIA FORTIER

Corporate Board Member and Senior
Fellow, Graduate School of International
Affairs, University of Ottawa
Former Canadian Ambassador
Location: Ottawa, Ontario, Canada

MY HIGHEST PROFESSIONAL ACHIEVEMENTS

1. In the Canadian Foreign Service: As chief adviser for the Organization of American States (OAS) High Level Mission to Perú, helping the Peruvians negotiate a peaceful end to a crisis, hold the state together during the fall of a corrupt government, form an interim government, disband a brutal secret service, reform the electoral law and institutions, and finally observe fair and transparent elections
2. As Canadian Ambassador in the Dominican Republic, providing the idea and support for a first-ever referendum by poor communities to approve or disapprove of a multibillion-dollar Canadian mining project
3. After retirement, making the transition to the private sector with directorships on two Canadian companies of integrity in the international resource sector (mining and renewable natural gas)

STUMBLING BLOCKS OR STEPPING-STONES

Patricia Fortier's life so far has been the kind of adventure that movies are made of, and as a result, there is a warmth and wisdom about her that make you feel that if only you had an afternoon to sit down with her, you would learn so much about life and work and the many political under-takings around the world. She grew up in a very small town called Pine Falls, in Northern Manitoba, Canada. With only 600 people in the whole village, there wasn't even a traffic light, and the high school needed every kid (including the boy with a leg brace) to put together a football team. But this small town wasn't average. Because of the pulp and paper indus-try, the people of the town had good union jobs and were also attuned to world markets. There were some in the small community who traveled and worked in various countries. They came back and sparked the idea among young people that there was something out there. In fact, several decided to see what they could do both for and beyond Canada. Out of that small town, there were four people who went into Canadian foreign service and three who became ambassadors, including Patricia.

After high school, Patricia attended a year of university before she and her older sister Verla realized they were both restless and, with their parents' blessing, headed off to Europe. Sometimes decisions are made with unknown consequences. Verla ended up traveling through Iran, Afghanistan, and India, while Patricia ended up hitchhiking through the Sahara Desert and became fascinated by Africa. That experience changed both of their lives and perhaps the life of their youngest sister as well. (Gail heard the stories and became an artist.) Back from her travels, Patricia chose to pursue a degree in African history at Queen's University in Kingston, Ontario, and then followed with a master's in public admin-istration. In the 1980s oil boom in Alberta, she worked in hospitals, the legislature, and provincial government, and finally looked set to stay as an urban transportation planner in city government.

Until one night at a party, a friend asked her to accompany him when he sat for the Canadian Foreign Service exam. She said yes but made a decision. Since she would be there anyway, she would write the exam too. She was successful. That year, 3,000 young Canadians took that exam, and 27 became foreign service officers. During her training in Ottawa, Patricia met Paul, who was also in the foreign service, and they fell in love just before her first posting to Kenya. Off she went, and for two years they courted, Nairobi to Ottawa, by letter and infrequent visits, no internet, terrible phone lines, and expensive air travel. They arranged joint postings in India and were finally married while on holiday in Australia. Patricia and Paul became a team, one of the pioneer "employee couples" in the Canadian Foreign Service. They supported each other in life and in their careers and both became ambassadors.

Patricia had 10 postings around the world, in Africa, Asia, and the Americas, including three in the United States. On 9/11, she had recently arrived at her posting as head of the Political Section in the Canadian Embassy in Washington, DC. Inside the embassy at the time, she was close enough to see the smoke rise and feel the ground shake when one plane hit the Pentagon. For the plane that was still in the air, the embassy on Pennsylvania Avenue was positioned exactly in between two likely targets, the White House and the Capitol Building. When the brave passengers of Flight 93 sacrificed their lives to save others, Patricia and her embassy colleagues were deeply moved and personally thankful for the act that may have saved their lives.

Her last postings were as Canadian Ambassador to the Dominican Republic (DR), then to Perú and Bolivia. In the DR, she was involved in a huge new Canadian mining operation (the indigenous peoples were mining gold in that particular location before Columbus arrived), but it would have an impact on several small communities. Her experience in democracy-building and her leadership created the momentum and support for a community referendum where everyone, including the poorest of those communities, was assured of a voice. Earlier in her career, she had been entranced by the democratic will of the Peruvian people when she had worked as chief adviser to the OAS High Level Mission, which was charged with enabling a return to democracy in Perú after a fraudulent election. So, having observed Bolivian elections with the

Inter-American Institute of Human Rights, she jumped at the chance to become Canadian Ambassador to Perú and to Bolivia.

On return from this last time as Ambassador, she undertook the role of Assistant Deputy Minister in Global Affairs Canada, equivalent to Assistant Secretary in the US State Department. In this job, Patricia was responsible for all consular affairs—emergency management for any crisis globally and security for every embassy abroad and the offices in Canada—basically any bad thing that happened in the world that affected her fellow citizens. At the same time, she was the operational lead for global embassy operations in support of a massive Syrian refugee movement to Canada. Her political masters, Ministers and Prime Minister, were newly elected and therefore sometimes nervous but very supportive, and she had great staff and colleagues. There were many sleepless nights and very few free weekends, but the work was never boring.

At this peak of her career, Patricia's husband began to feel unwell. Strange health problems arose. They didn't know what it was. Having lived and worked with each other for 30 years around the globe, Patricia and Paul were sensitive to each other. Something was wrong. One night, Patricia suddenly woke up, looked at Paul sleeping, and thought, "What am I doing?" Her work was important to Canadian diplomats, to Canadian citizens abroad, and to the Canadian government, but no one is irreplaceable. After that waking night, she knew she had to make time to be with Paul.

Patricia had learned a lesson in crises, especially in consular affairs, with people at risk, that sometimes you just have to make a decision that will change your life for somebody else's life. And that is what she did. She retired from her government position, significantly reduced her workload, and took a seat on a corporate board in the private sector.

A few months later, the diagnosis came. Paul had ALS, also called Lou Gehrig's disease, a progressive illness with a terminal prognosis and a very limited timeframe. As she and Paul adjusted to the news, Paul was insistent that she continue to build a life, one that would go into the future after he was no longer with her. She wanted only to be by his side, but he knew her well, and he did not relent. While supporting Paul emotionally and physically, she pushed herself to engage with the corporate board, the university, and volunteer projects.

As the disease progressed, Paul was able to do things one day, and the next day he could not, so the two of them would sit down as they always had, talk it over, and make decisions together. Meanwhile, Paul was considering another decision. Shortly after his diagnosis, the Canadian Parliament had passed medical aid in dying (MAID) legislation, which allows people who are terminally ill and whose death is reasonably foreseeable to choose when and how they die. ALS made Paul a candidate, and he was thinking about this very seriously. He and Patricia had many difficult conversations; it was hard to accept. Paul was strong in his knowledge of his body and mind, and he was brave in facing up to the reality. He decided that MAID was what he wanted. For Patricia he had put off this decision longer than he might have and now was suffering, so it would be very soon…in days. He said his farewells to his siblings and to his many friends. As the hours ticked by, Patricia didn't think she could go through with it, but when the time came, she opened the door and she welcomed the doctors in. That evening Paul was able to have a drink with his children and say goodbye. He then walked up the stairs, leaning on Patricia. The doctor set up and asked the question; Paul said yes, thanked him, and then he died, as he wished—at home, in the arms of his love.

Leaving her high-level government position had been a shock and was disorienting for her identity, but losing her life's love and companion was grief and loss beyond anything Patricia had ever known. She was thankful that Paul had known she had to build a life for the future. She made it through those early days with the help of her family, friends, work, and the local ALS Society bereavement group. Many friends, some she had not known well, surprised her by going beyond expectations in care and support. She welcomed hugs and company. At present in her corporate, academic, and voluntary work, she works with old friends, has made new friends, is constantly surprised by her students' new thoughts, and is working in organizations where her experience is useful; but the learning curve can be steep. She is engaged with her community, her country, and the world once more.

While she still misses Paul every morning and night, it does not stop her from living, and Paul would approve. She managed crises when lives could be lost by one bad decision. She understands it personally, with the loss of someone so precious and dear to her. Now Patricia savors life in a way that many do not. She knows we may not have tomorrow, and each day, she decides to live with intention and joy. At the end of the day, she will tell you, love helps.

WORDS OF WISDOM FROM PATRICIA TO YOU

- Talk to people who are going or have gone through the same thing you are experiencing. They are also trying to figure out how to accept and grow in changed lives. You can help each other make sense of this new world.
- If you're in a crisis, making a critical decision, or taking on a difficult endeavor, breathe first and then understand that everyone with you is also trying to breathe. Look around and support others in small ways. If you or someone else makes a mistake, well at least we all tried, together.
- Take your concerns and channel them into energy; do something useful. Love helps.

Overcoming Cancer

Patricia Rodriguez Christian

CEO at CRC Group and Texas Standard
Commercial Construction
Location: Dallas, Texas, United States

My Highest Achievements

1. Founder of CRC Group
2. Survived acute lymphoblastic leukemia (ALL)
3. A member of the founding group of WomenExecs on Boards

Stumbling Blocks or Stepping-Stones

When Patricia Christian stepped onto the Harvard campus in 2016 to attend the WomenExecs on Boards corporate governance program, she joined 67 other high-level women from 17 countries who all had a vision of attaining corporate board seats. But Patricia was also fulfilling a life dream that she had to step foot on the Harvard campus. She wanted to do it for herself, and she wanted to model lifelong learning for her teenage son, which had become of prime importance due to recent events in her life. Looking back, it's something to imagine all the motivations and dynamics behind the women around the semicircle seating in the

Harvard Business School classroom. One wonders how many more like Patricia had layers of motivation far beyond the initial icebreaker, share-session conversation?

Patricia was one whose layers ran deep. She arrived a successful CEO of two companies in Dallas, Texas. One was in construction, and one was in business process outsourcing. Entrepreneurship was in her blood, as her parents had always made their own way, and her mother had always encouraged her to find a way to stand on her own. Early on, Patricia grasped this concept and set out to create her own independence.

After a short start at a local community college, she moved from the border town of El Paso, Texas, to Albuquerque, New Mexico. Her family couldn't afford to pay for her college, so Patricia went to work full-time and took courses at night. This was a difficult period, but the mental fortitude Patricia gained in these years would be paramount in the years to come.

An early adapter, Patricia founded her first business supporting multilingual and bilingual communities in the Spanish language. The work was rewarding in its mission, but she was living out of a suitcase. She traveled all week, would come home and unpack on Saturday, and regroup and then head back out Sunday morning. A weary road warrior, she decided to sell the business and go to graduate school full-time at the University of New Mexico.

Afterward, Patricia did a short run in a Fortune 100 company before realizing that navigating a big corporate behemoth was not for her. She left and soon found herself consulting with the United States Department of Commerce and was recruited to work there full-time, building an initiative to pair underserved, minority-focused universities with the resources of the federal government. It was innovative, entre-preneurial, and exciting, but as fate would have it, Patricia met Larry, the founder of Texas Standard Commercial Construction in Dallas, Texas.

Patricia and Larry soon found the distance too far, and Patricia took a leave of absence and moved to Texas. However, appropriate-level openings were few and far between, and eventually she resigned and founded CRC Group; there she acquired, turned around, and sold mul-tiple businesses, in addition to serving on the board of Women's Business

Enterprise National Council (WBENC), the premier certifying entity for small, women-owned businesses. This organization provides a designation designed to help women business owners receive an improved level of corporate and government business. She also became a real estate broker and personally manages the family's real estate holdings.

At an inflection point, Patricia and Larry realized that her visionary and strategic mindset was exactly what Texas Standard needed, and she became the CEO. Patricia has always been a visionary. She remembers standing in the kitchen as an 11-year-old girl listening to her mother attempt to teach her how to cook. Frustrated and bored, Patricia finally spoke up and let her mother know that she didn't need to learn how to cook because when she grew up, she was going to hire someone to do it for her. Her mother accepted her resolve, embraced the vision, and never tried to teach Patricia how to cook again.

Ever the visionary, Patricia set her sights on a future for the CRC Group and went to work building a team. The team is passionate and talented, and Patricia helped them get into the right places in the company to exercise their best strengths. She was doing it because that's what she did as a business owner. Although it all became fateful, when suddenly this team needed more than anyone expected. Patricia was diagnosed with leukemia, and the world turned upside down. Shocked but resilient, Patricia didn't take long to set a personal vision, and that was survival. She determined to avoid her normally data-driven methods and looked at only one mental picture, making it through to recovery.

Patricia met with her team and told them the diagnosis and that she needed to take time off to focus on getting well. They stepped up and stepped in and even managed to surprise Patricia with their skills, dedication, and success. In fact, when it was all said and done, they had outperformed the previous year.

A surprise support system came from the WBENC network, where the women who were most involved surrounded Patricia with support, sending cards, books, emails, and letters. They lifted her spirits and gave her much-needed energy to keep going.

Larry, her husband of over 20 years, stepped in to take care of the household and parenting. Patricia had one job, and everyone agreed it was to get well. And she did get well. When she took her first step on the Harvard campus, it was more meaningful than she had ever imagined, as she was less than one year into her recovery from leukemia. She had fulfilled a dream and was ready to set her sights on a new and exciting vision for the future. Little did she know that by 2020 she would not only be serving on corporate boards but also fulfilling her innate need to serve the underserved by co-leading the network formed out of that initial Harvard program. Today, Patricia's legacy continues to grow as she advances the state of gender equality in the boardroom and procurement opportunities for women-owned businesses.

WORDS OF WISDOM FROM PATRICIA TO YOU

- I want to encourage you to be confident in your point of view. Do not suppress it, because it comes from within you. Bring all your authentic self to the table. You do not need to be like someone else to be successful. In fact, trying to be like someone else is neither fun nor likely to succeed. You have something important to add to the world. Bring that.
- And this is important: Choose the right partner. It took me a long time to find Larry, but when I did, I knew I had the right one. He gets me. I can be all of me, and we have always been really good partners.

Lynda Bourque Moss

Former Montana State Senator and CEO
at Moss Consulting
Location: Billings, Montana, United States

My Highest Achievements

1. Served in many jobs and on many boards: My career spans 30-plus years and weaves together work in public policy, non-profit management, philanthropy, and business development. I have served as an executive, state senator, founder, board member, and now as board chair of the Northwest Area Foundation. I serve as a board member of Montana State Fund, the worker's compensation program for Montana, and I am a trustee on the American Craft Council, a national organization supporting craft artists in the US. Previously I have served on the American Museum Association, International Council of Museum board of directors as well as many statewide nonprofit organizations.

2. Enjoyed a wide variety of organizations: As the executive director for a regional museum and a small foundation, I have been responsible for staff ranging from 2 to 25, however in all my work, I was able to expand each organization. For my board

responsibilities, I serve on the Northwest Area Foundation with assets of $450 million.

3. Wrote a children's book, *A Montana Love Story*

STUMBLING BLOCKS OR STEPPING-STONES

On Lynda's office shelf is *A Montana Love Story*, the children's book she wrote based on the true adventures of a tiny dog, a pygmy goat, and a Labrador retriever. The story is a great metaphor for Lynda's journey, a journey where friends and family helped her find her way when she was lost and couldn't do it on her own. It's just one of the beautiful things that came out of Lynda's pain as she grieved the loss of a loved one.

Lynda is a creative. She has always loved the arts, as an observer and as an artist and a writer, so it's no surprise that her career began in the art world. After completing a master's in fine arts, Lynda went to work in a gallery, followed by other galleries. Through her passion for the arts, she soon became a leader and began to learn the skills needed to turn the love of art into sustainable business models. As her skills progressed, her responsibilities increased until she found herself interviewing for the role to lead a history museum called the Western Heritage Center. The question that ultimately tipped the scales in her favor for the position was when the interviewer asked her how she felt about history. Her honest answer was that most of it was really boring. That clinched the job.

Lynda's mandate then became to make sure the museum wasn't boring. In doing so, Lynda learned the importance of working with communities, listening to the people, and learning from their stories in order to create programs that emphasize people coming together. Being a part of the art world also taught her about visionary leadership. The concept of imagining the future, continuously adapting by overcoming perceived barriers, and allowing for change are all synchronous with leadership and art. In fact, leadership is very much about art.

These skills would become crucial to her success as she began to turn her eye toward politics. While continuing her work in community initiatives and the arts, Lynda was recruited to run for a state legislative house seat in Montana. Her life's mantra is to never say no. So, she said yes, ran for office, and lost. Disappointed but willing to take it as a learning journey, Lynda continued with the arts. She had ambitions, but she was happy, and life was progressing nicely until tragedy struck and her husband was killed in a tragic one-person car accident. Lynda had one great love in her life from high school sweetheart to now, and he was it. The loss was sudden, tragic, and shocking.

In a daze for almost two years afterward, Lynda relied on friends and family to keep moving forward. She had been spun into a world where she felt that she didn't know anything anymore. It was so painful and confusing that she experienced what the medical field calls broken-heart syndrome, which is a physical pain and shortness of breath brought on by extreme emotion and stress. Emotionally and literally, her heart hurt.

As she relied on others, she learned to be comfortable being vulnerable, not because she was brave, but because she couldn't do anything else. She also knew that she had to move forward. She had to reimagine her future and put together a new path, which she did over time. Her new path began to bring together all her experiences and provided the new opportunities that she needed to have a happy and successful life despite the devastating turn in her journey.

During this two-year period, she kept following her mantra of never saying no and went on trips to South America, China, and the Outer Banks of North Carolina. And, once again, she was recruited for a legislature seat in the senate for the state of Montana. This time she won and went on to serve two terms as Secretary and Vice Chair of the Legislative Audit Committee, successfully passing legislation linking state policies with corporate and nonprofit organizations and serving on the Montana State Fund board, a workers compensation fund with assets of over $1.4 billion.

Unable to run for a third term due to term limits, Lynda continued her work in philanthropy, building international partnerships linking indigenous youth in Montana and Patagonia before founding her own business, serving the community, and, as always, enjoying and creating the arts.

Today, there is a richness to Lynda's journey, a savoring of the moments and relationships and an ongoing desire to do things that matter. At every opportunity, Lynda tries to understand what is needed and then to create that for herself and for others. A beautiful part of her legacy is now painted on the walls of the Montana State Capitol building, honoring women as community builders, a contribution that came out of Lynda's heart and imagination as she walked the halls during her legislative tenure.

As she served on the judiciary committee, which is quite formal and oversees all the policy decisions, Lynda would watch and listen to the women who came to testify. They were mothers and daughters and sisters and grandmothers. Lynda thought about them and wondered if any of those women and girls could see themselves inside the state capitol. As she walked the halls during the day, she was attuned to the artwork, and something was bothering her about it. Finally, she realized what it was. There seemed to be a lack of female representation in the art. She decided to follow this nagging and walked around the capitol counting the images of human beings. The final tally was 40 men and 7 women, five of whom were the same woman, Sacagawea.

She decided that for the women and girls who were coming into the capitol to ever see themselves working there, they needed to see themselves in the art. Lynda wanted to open their imagination and give them the power to investigate the future and think about the possibilities. It took some work, but Lynda was able to get a bill passed that established a mural and lead the fundraising. Today, as women and girls walk the halls of the capitol, they will see people who look like them, living and working in community and government and ultimately making a difference for others.

Words of Wisdom from Lynda to You

- If you experience a great loss, be brave, share your grief, and step back into the world with the help of your networks and friends. Rekindle your sense of humor, be creative, and celebrate each day.
- When you step into a new opportunity, come with wide eyes. You need to be able to see what is in front of you but also what is around you, be aware of the periphery. If you know what's going on around the edges and in the distance, you can think about its impact on the decisions and sustainability of whatever you are doing.
- Be open to possibilities. There can be something very helpful in whatever opportunity emerges that you could be part of, and it may take you to places that you had never imagined yourself going. You will learn from all those experiences.

CONCLUSION

Dear Reader,

The stories that you've read are about real leaders dealing with real life. The struggles that they faced and the ones that you will face on the path to any worthwhile achievement are not abnormal. They are the norm. And it is in the struggle that you will become strong.

Real leadership is often about the behind-the-scenes things that go on that we don't really talk about. It's the showing up for work and giving 100 percent, paying attention to every person who comes to the office, and thinking thoroughly about how to make the workplace better for all those lives that you touch that day, the employees, the customers, and the vendors. And sometimes, it's doing all of that on only a couple of hours of sleep, because at home your loved one is dying or your son is on drugs or your daughter is going through an eating disorder or your spouse is leaving or your parents are sick or you, like Susan Brock, PhD, mentioned in the beginning, are going through cancer treatment. Sometimes, it's holding your head up and making decisions even though your boss is questioning the job that you're doing, or you are preparing to layoff part of your team that you care for deeply and who you need to get the work done. It's getting up when you feel defeated and then getting up again the next day and the next.

Often, only those who are closest, only a handful of people, know the struggles behind the scenes, because leadership means that you're there for other people. It means a giving of yourself to others when you're tired, when you're sick, and when you're not sure you can keep going. Leadership is grit and heart and strength. It means overcoming life's greatest disappointments, challenges, and tragedies to give others hope, direction, encouragement, and guidance. It's taking those life events that have given you your strongest emotions and channeling that emotion into something good.

People need leadership, and you can be the leader they need.

Just keep getting up, so that one day, your story will be the one that makes a lasting difference in the lives of others. So climb to your greatest potential (which is always more than you think it is), and as you're climbing, leave the ladder down to help bring others up behind you.

We hope that on your darkest days, you will remember that you are not alone, that we, the members of the WomenExecs on Boards network, will be somewhere on the sidelines, watching anxiously, sending you good-energy vibes, and cheering wildly as you take your place in the leadership arena. We will be there as you fight and fall and get back up to keep fighting. So, don't give up.

Your Raving Fans,
Bonnie, Lisa, and the Members of
WomenExecs on Boards

Would you like your people to read this book?

If you would like to discuss how you could bring these ideas to your team, we would love to hear from you. Our titles are available at competitive discounts when purchased in bulk across both physical and digital formats. We can offer bespoke editions featuring corporate logos, customized covers, or letters from company directors in the front matter can also be created in line with your special requirements.

We work closely with leading experts and organizations to bring forward-thinking ideas to a global audience. Our books are designed to help you be more successful in work and life.

For further information, or to request a catalogue, please contact: **business@johnmurrays.co.uk**
sales-US@nicholasbrealey.com (North America only)

Nicholas Brealey Publishing is an imprint of John Murray Press.